MAKING FAMILIES WORK

*A New Search for Christian
Family Values*

MARGARET GRIMER

GEOFFREY
CHAPMAN

Geoffrey Chapman
A Cassell imprint
Villiers House, 41/47 Strand, London, WC2N 5JE
387 Park Avenue South, New York 10016–8810

First published 1994

British Library Cataloguing-in-Publication Data
A catalogue record for this book is available from the British Library.

Library of Congress Cataloging-in-Publication Data
Applied for.

ISBN 0–225–66722–3

Photograph of the author on back cover by Top Floor Studio, Woodbridge.
Excerpts from the Jerusalem Bible, copyright © 1966 by
Darton, Longman & Todd Ltd and Doubleday,
a division of Bantam Doubleday Dell Publishing Group, Inc.
Reprinted by permission.

Typeset by Intype, London
Printed and bound in Great Britain by
Biddles Ltd, Guildford and King's Lynn

CONTENTS

ACKNOWLEDGEMENTS

I should like to thank those experienced people who generously read the script and offered me many helpful suggestions: Bishop Christopher Budd, the staffs of One Plus One and of the Catholic Marriage Advisory Council (CMAC), Hilary Elliott of the Institute of Contemporary Spirituality and my friends of the Arc Ecumenical Community at Oxford.

I am grateful to those who over the years have shared with me the story of their family lives: the clients of CMAC, parish marriage teams throughout the country, couples preparing for marriage, and young men from Hollesley Bay Prison and Young Offenders Institution.

Special thanks are due to my friend and former CMAC colleague Anthony Ford. Anthony is a parish priest at Tolworth, and if this book succeeds in being user-friendly to parish groups it is thanks to his unique blend of enthusiasm, insistence and inspiration.

FOREWORD

It is often said that one of the reasons marriages and families fail so quickly is that nobody tells young people that you need to work at them as soon as relationships begin. The idea of work, especially if qualified by 'hard', may sound thoroughly daunting and certainly less than romantic!

Margaret Grimer addresses this issue in a practical way, not endorsing the despair that can so often accompany such comments, but looking at the values and skills that are needed if marriages and families are to flourish.

On p. 94 of the book we find a list of ten family values for today. If these are to be successfully turned into values of particular families, we need to learn how to handle them and let them become the basis of marriage and family life. *Making Families Work* is an attempt to enable people to achieve this.

This is a book not just for beginners, but also for those who have already lived many years in marriage and family. These latter can contribute richly to the process from their own well-developed skills and values in managing the joys and sorrows already experienced. I hope it will also encourage those whose marriages and families have failed for whatever reason. They have much to share, learnt not in the school of success but in the more humbling school of failure.

Central to this book is prayer. It is not an activity into which we escape from the unbearable, but a place where we meet the living God in whose presence we can own all the things happening in our lives, good and bad, joyful and sorrowful, bearable and unbearable.

In the list of family values to which I have already referred, you will find **truth** (recognizing and naming what is happening); **trust** (the affirmation of important relationships); **courage** (staying with the hard things); **service** (looking outward); **joy** (delighting in the good); **love** (reflecting the living God). All these values can be woven together as prayer, and will lie at the heart of marriage and family.

I hope that this book will help many people to live their most important relationships in a way that is truthful, prayerful, loving and enriching.

Christopher Budd
Bishop of Plymouth

A WEDDING TRANSFORMED

Three days later there was a wedding at Cana in Galilee. The mother of Jesus was there, and Jesus and his disciples had also been invited.

When they ran out of wine, since the wine provided for the wedding was all finished, the mother of Jesus said to him, 'They have no wine'. Jesus said, 'Woman, why turn to me? My hour has not come yet.'

His mother said to the servants, 'Do whatever he tells you'. There were six stone water jars standing there, meant for the ablutions that are customary among the Jews: each could hold twenty or thirty gallons.

Jesus said to the servants, 'Fill the jars with water', and they filled them to the brim. 'Draw some out now' he told them 'and take it to the steward.' They did this; the steward tasted the water, and it had turned into wine.

Having no idea where it came from—only the servants who had drawn the water knew—the steward called the bridegroom and said, 'People generally serve the best wine first, and keep the cheaper sort till the guests have had plenty to drink; but you have kept the best wine till now'.

This was the first of the signs given by Jesus: it was given at Cana in Galilee. He let his glory be seen, and his disciples believed in him.

John 2

Chapter 1

WHY TURN TO ME?

The news that day forced me to face it. International and political news had been dropped from the TV headlines. Instead came three stories. One was of a two-year-old boy in Liverpool, enticed away while his mother shopped and later found dead beside a railway. Two people were arrested. They were both ten years old.

Next came news of an eleven-year-old girl. She had been left alone in a London flat while her single mother was taking a holiday in Spain. Then followed an item about new regulations to ensure that absent fathers pay towards their children's support.

Three items. Each in some way about the family. Each, at first sight anyway, telling of something which should never have happened if families were carrying out their expected roles.

I am familiar with family breakdown. I brought up my children in London where many rootless people drift. I taught in an Inner London comprehensive where two parents at home were never taken for granted. I worked with the Catholic Marriage Advisory Council which counsels individuals and couples with marriage difficulties.

I live in a country where divorce is widespread and where nearly 40 per cent of existing marriages are expected to end in divorce. This affects all levels of society: three of our Queen's children have married in a glare of publicity; in a glare of publicity all three marriages have failed.

Yet somehow I thought of all these breakdowns as exceptions. It was sad that marriage and family relationships had become so fragile—and we should all work to minimize the hurt—but marriage and family were still the norm. Then I watched the news on that day in 1993 and with heart-stopping vertigo my suppositions stood on their head.

Those three news items forced me to face up to the possibility that perhaps family breakdown is so widespread and so severe that it is not the exception now but the rule. Do we still expect most families to carry out the basic roles of providing for children, keeping them safe and bringing them up to choose right from wrong? Can we go on taking this for granted?

The breakdown of families causes suffering and pain to many individuals; the breakdown of the family system would threaten the very cohesion of our society. In the face of such a threat it is common to fly to religion.

Two cries are heard. One goes along the lines of: 'Divorce is too easy. Marriage should be for life. Bring back Christian marriage!' The other runs: 'People have grown selfish. Where's their sense of duty? Bring back Christian family values!'

These are understandable reactions. If men and women always wanted to stay married, and if people were always willing to place the collective family good before their individual needs, neither marriage nor family would be so fragile. And since people seem no longer willing, something must make them. Where else can we look for such a moral imperative if not to the Christian churches?

Yet the Christian churches too are afraid. They too feel the erosion of what are sometimes called 'Christian family values'. It may be hard to say exactly what these are, but the church senses that if they are lost we shall lose something valuable to everybody.

The churches have another fear. Even if they rediscover Christian family values, they are afraid that most people, and especially most young people, will find these cherished values irrelevant. If you used to have a starring role it is hard to discover that what is being enacted now is a different play in a different place. As the future of the family is played out, what will be the churches' role? Hand-wringing audience? Spear carrier? Or is there yet an important part for the Christian churches to play in the next act of the family saga?

The churches are somewhat perplexed about their role here. Maybe we are over-reacting if a few dramatic incidents make us fear that society itself is falling apart. Yet how should we respond to the increased breakdown of some families and to the increased fragility of all families? Are we powerless in the grip of inexorable social trends? Is it even our place to support the family? As Jesus said when a wedding went wrong, 'Why turn to me?'

This book asserts that the Christian churches can make a valuable contribution to family survival and happiness. Just as

Jesus at Cana did make a couple's happiness his business and effect a transformation, so the Christian churches have it within their grasp to transform the way families live today.

A Year of the Family gives the Christian churches an opportunity to look afresh at what is happening to the family. It is a chance for us to look again at the values Christians hold, and to see whether any can be relied upon to help us understand and live our family lives. If we discover such values, it is then for us to decide how they are to be drawn upon for the benefit of all—as the servants drew superlative wine at Cana and transformed the prospects for a young married couple.

I propose two guides for this quest. The first is experience of families: your family and mine, families we know, families we have heard about and encountered, families present in our neighbourhoods and congregations. It is important for our notion of family to be grounded in reality, to be recognizable and realizable in day-to-day family life.

The second guide comes from our understanding of the Kingdom preached by Jesus Christ. This understanding will be different for every Christian, but my own thoughts about Christ's Kingdom as I read the gospels may help to trigger yours.

It is likely that my view will be coloured by my Roman Catholic spectacles, since I am a lifelong member of that Christian tradition. Yet most of my experience is with families who would see themselves as far from the Roman Catholic ideal, and over a lifetime I have spent much more energy explaining them to the institutional church than ever I spent expounding the institutional church to them. If my assumptions do not exactly fit other Christian traditions I would ask you to make your own substitutions: in this way many different Christian churches can use the Year of the Family to take a fresh look at Christian family values.

As a child I shuffled cards clumsily, until one marvellous day my young brother split the pack in two, laid both halves on the table, grasped the corners of each between a finger and thumb, and with a flick interleaved one half-pack with the other. This is the way I shall try to use our two guides: to alternate between lived experience of family and the values of Christ's Kingdom, until a whole is formed in which both are fully represented.

If you would like to go further and pray about the family, either by yourself or in church groups, this book offers a way of doing that. People pray differently, and for Christians every

way is valid if it brings us nearer to Christ. The way I choose
in this book is the way of story, imagination and fantasy, because
it encourages us to make use of our personal feelings and experience in families. Our own family story is the one in which we
are the experts.

Each chapter, then, ends with a 'Taking stock' section, which
suggests meditation and prayer based on a story from the gospels. You can, if you choose, skip these and read on but I
venture to suggest that you will get more from the book if you
try them out. If you are prepared to return to them several
times the yield will be even greater. Those sections are rounded
off with a few thoughts to encourage you to reflect on your
own experience of family in the light of the gospel.

The gospel sections from each chapter can be used as part
of the agenda for church gatherings of ordinary people, who,
increasingly, are meeting to think and pray about the family.
The chapter 'For group leaders' at the end of the book offers
suggestions for running such groups, together with agendas and
summaries of the main ideas for each meeting.

Perhaps the first Christian family value we should try for is
readiness to admit that our families are not perfect. Christopher
Budd, the Roman Catholic bishop responsible for speaking on
marriage and family life, acknowledges that families need their
privacy but points out that respectability can cut us off from
the community.

> We have to break through the destructive protective barrier that
> respectability often puts up, with catastrophic effects on family
> life. We need to be at ease, admitting that things are not going well
> and get beyond the 'we mustn't let the neighbours know' attitude
> that can be so damaging. We can do this by building up a
> widespread acceptance that there is no such thing as the perfect
> family.
>
> There will always be problems and this fact does not reflect bad
> parenting. But if we are more realistic in presenting family life,
> instead of preaching unattainable perfection, we may change the
> way we think into something more helpful.

Coming from a tradition that does not allow divorce, I may
perhaps use divorce to illustrate the need for admitting family
failings. Research shows that the divorce rate of one in three is
just as high in families that call themselves Christian. So it is a
safe bet that if it has not happened to your marriage it has

happened to your brother or sister, to your parents or your cousins, to your uncle or aunt, to your son or to your daughter. Divorce happens in clergy families, in ministers' families, to the relatives of celibate nuns, priests and bishops. As I write, the marriage of one of my own children is breaking down, and it breaks my heart. Divorce is a fact of life and a fact of Christian life, and it is a great relief if Christians can admit this freely in their communities.

Many families with other difficulties suffer quite needlessly from the feeling that they cannot tell fellow Christians what their life is really like, that 'if they knew they wouldn't accept me'. Somehow we must build up a widespread acceptance that the church is the church of sinners and is not just for the righteous and successful, which is why I propose *admitting* family failings as our first Christian family value.

All of us have imperfect families. Are you sometimes resentful or bitter at the way your parents treated you? Are you ever depressed or furious at your partner's attitudes? Are you distressed or angry at your children's behaviour? Every Christian community needs to ensure that its members can feel comfortable in admitting their own and their family's shortcomings freely. As Christopher Budd says:

> It is important to accept people as they are. That doesn't mean to say that we haven't got any beliefs and values. It just says that if someone is in a mess we accept them in the mess that they are in, and work within that framework. It is as simple and as difficult as that.

Taking stock

The parable of the Pharisee and the Tax Collector can be used as a way of starting to pray that Christians may create an atmosphere where *admitting* family failings becomes possible and natural.

Becoming quiet

In preparation for the story it helps to allow yourself to relax. Let your mind grow still, and your thoughts quiet. Breathe slowly and easily. Let the worries and cares of the day drop away with each breath out. God is all around you. Breathe in God . . .

The grace

Before you read the story you may like to ask that it may shed light on the theme of this chapter.

Father, help us to feel safe enough to admit to the failings in our family. Help us to know that you accept and love us just as we are, with all our faults.

The story

Two men went up to the Temple to pray, one a Pharisee, the other a tax collector. The Pharisee stood there and said this prayer to himself, 'I thank you, God, that I am not grasping, unjust, adulterous like the rest of mankind, and particularly that I am not like this tax collector here. I fast twice a week; I pay tithes on all I get.' The tax collector stood some distance away, not daring even to raise his eyes to heaven; but he beat his breast and said, 'God, be merciful to me, a sinner'. This man, I tell you, went home again at rights with God; the other did not. For everyone who exalts himself will be humbled, but the man who humbles himself will be exalted.

Bringing it home

Before you visualize the scene, remind yourself of the reputation of tax collectors. They are collaborators with the Roman occupying forces. They exact protection money for their bosses. They terrorize small traders. They take their own cut. Some people say they mock their victims by sleeping with their wives. They are despicable, a symptom of everything that is wrong with the country. Pharisees have the reputation for thinking religion very important and for keeping every religious law scrupulously.

Now visualize the Temple. What does it look like? How big is it? How is it decorated and furnished? Do not worry if a contemporary scene comes to your mind—this is your temple, you can furnish it any way you like. Is it crowded? Who is there: the Pharisee, the tax collector, anybody else? Have a good look at the people. Don't worry if they are dressed in twentieth-century clothes, you can imagine them how you like. Where are they standing? What about the sounds? And the smells?

Now put yourself into the picture. You may be a Pharisee, or a tax collector, or some other visitor to the Temple. Who will you be? In a moment you are going to run through the story again. Let it unroll like a film in your mind. As it happens, try to notice how you feel: smug? angry? resentful? ashamed? or what? When the action is over have a conversation with Jesus, the storyteller. Tell him what you experienced, ask him anything you want, hear what Jesus says to you.

Some thoughts for today's families

Maybe 'being right with God' is not very much to do with managing to keep all the rules. What, then, makes families right with God?

There *are* people whose lifestyle seems to threaten family values. Who, for instance? Without analysing or judging your feelings about these people, perhaps you could take them to Jesus the storyteller from time to time during the next few days. Tell him how you feel about people who seem to threaten the family. Ask him to hold these feelings for you for the time being. Be confident that he will, bit by bit, show you how you can become 'right with God'.

During the next week you might try to take some small risk to be more open with others about your family circumstances. Notice whether that makes them more able to be open with you.

Chapter 2

WHO ARE MY MOTHER
AND MY BROTHERS?

Christians believe that Christ has set us free. If we are to enter
into that freedom within our churches we need to be free to tell
our fellow Christians when all is not well in our families. We
also need to know that we shall be heard with sympathy and
understanding. That is why I propose that the first Christian
family value for today should be admitting family failings. Our
churches can first of all be gatherings where our family's shortcomings can be freely acknowledged.

We may find ourselves in good company. What sort of family
member was Jesus? I tried to imagine his early ministry through
the eyes of his family, and came up with this poem.

Black sheep of the family

James and Joset and Jude and Simon
What has your brother done?

Brought all the riff-raff home, they say,
Fishermen swearing, clerks in the way,
Mad people raving, crazy as he,
Prostitutes preening and calling for tea.
Let's get his sisters to take him in hand,
Tell him these rave-ups have got to be banned.

James and Joset and Jude and Simon
Where has your brother gone?

Slumming in some low dive, they say,
Tried to get near him, crowds blocked the way.
Sent in a message 'Come out here to us—
Your mother, your sisters—we won't make a fuss'.
Said *they're* his family now, wouldn't shift,
Started no end of a family rift.

James and Joset and Jude and Simon
Where is your brother now?

Down at the synagogue teaching, they say,
Carpenter's tools here all rusting away,
Shaming the family, playing the quack,
Can't even fix our poor neighbour's bad back.
Where did he get it from? Trust him? No fear!
Nothing religious could start off from here.

James and Joset and Jude and Simon
What if your brother's right?

Life would be changed in an instant, they say,
Demons that trouble us named, sent away.
Withered hands straightened and leprous limbs clean.
Fear like the raging sea stilled. Blind eyes keen . . .

Enough of this Kingdom enchantment, my lad,
Stick to the carpentry. Brother, you're mad!

It seems that Jesus behaved in a way that very much embarrassed his family. Here is Mark's account.

> He went home again, and once more such a crowd collected
> that they could not even have a meal. When his relatives
> heard of this, they set out to take charge of him, convinced
> he was out of his mind. . . . His mother and brothers now
> arrived and, standing outside, sent in a message asking for
> him. A crowd was sitting round him at the time the
> message was passed to him, 'Your mother and brothers and
> sisters are outside asking for you'. He replied, 'Who are
> my mother and my brothers?' And looking round at those
> sitting in a circle about him, he said, 'Here are my mother
> and my brothers. Anyone who does the will of God, that
> person is my brother and sister and mother.'

> Mark 3

'Who are my mother and my brothers?' asked Jesus. If we want
to understand what is happening to the family today we had
better define our terms. Who belongs to your family?

Everyone knows what a family is, yet the concept of family is
slippery. There is the nuclear family of mother, father and their
children. I have belonged to two of these: as a child with my
father and mother and my two brothers; as an adult with
my husband, our three sons and our daughter.

Now that these children have left our home they link us to

our extended family, which includes our son- and daughters-in-law and our seven grandchildren. My own grandparents died before I was born, so I had no experience of having a grandmother or grandfather; gradually I am discovering what being a grandparent can be like.

I am also rediscovering other members of my extended family. Here I am torn between my interest in people, which makes me want to know them better, and my fear of being overwhelmed by mutual hospitality and obligation. Brothers, cousins, nephews and nieces, and all their children, are out there somewhere, holding for me equal parts of threat and opportunity. Add the families of my son- and daughters-in-law, add my husband's relatives who are even more numerous than mine, and that's quite a lot of family.

But the concept of family is more slippery yet. Fifteen years of my life was spent as a full-time mother at home, but around that I had a varied working life as a social worker, a teacher, a voluntary group worker and then as a paid officer for the Catholic Marriage Advisory Council. The range of people I met in these different settings taught me to have no preconceptions about what constitutes a normal family, or so I supposed.

Nowadays I am increasingly involved as a chaplain visiting young men in prison. Most of their cells are decorated with family photographs. 'That's my Mum. He's my half-brother. She's my kid's mother. This is my girlfriend and her baby—no, he's not mine, he's her ex's. Here's our dog. This is my Dad, but he won't talk to me any more. That's my Nan when she married again.' And so it goes on: stepfamilies, blended families—some of his, some of hers, some of theirs—marriage, divorce, living together. Common-law wives, separated wives. Quarrelling, making up, parting, trying this, trying that. Some times it seems that the most permanent and stable member of the whole family is the dog. Certainly the very concept of family is stretched to breaking point. Perhaps we need to start again.

One of the minor puzzles of my childhood was how to explain the presence in our home of my mother's best friend. She lived with us, with my father and mother, my two brothers and myself. She was my godmother, we called her 'Auntie' yet she was no blood relation. She was, however, one of the family. I understood this, but I feared that nobody outside our family would understand and that we were somehow odd because of it.

I now have more experience of the variety of people who

can comprise a household or who come into those interwoven relationships of care and responsibility that people call their family. For years I lived in a suburban London street, and it was surprising how often I heard people there use the phrase 'one of the family'. A young mother said it about the elderly childless couple next door, a middle-aged woman said it of her Chinese lodger and a lonely widow said it of her cat. 'How's the family?' was sometimes answered in terms of nuclear or extended family, but just as often in terms of household or neighbours. Ties of blood or law frequently had less reality there than day-to-day caring and sharing.

I have found the same in prison. One young man was inconsolable because he was refused home leave to attend his mother's funeral. This was the woman who brought him up, who made the long, weary trek to see him every visiting day. So why the refusal? 'She's not my real Mum, of course. But she's been more of a Mum to me than my real Mum ever was.' Family is often where the heart is.

This concept of 'family by analogy' can sometimes be misused. I once attempted some education in relationships in a community home for young people with mental handicaps. I have changed its real name, but let us say that well-meaning persons were apt to refer to it as 'the family of Fatima House'. Together the young people and the staff and I tried to work out some ground rules for privacy and respect between men and women residents. One young woman lost no time in saying: 'They're not my family and he's not my brother. If he wants a kiss he can ask me nicely.' We Christians can use this concept of family by analogy very glibly, so that we speak readily of our parish family or the family of Christians. Making this family life a reality is more difficult.

It is clear that the concept of family can slide from nuclear to extended family, can embrace stepfamilies and blended families and can be adjusted to embrace households and neighbours. It can be trimmed to exclude relatives by blood or law but extended to include non-relatives who play a significant part in a person's life. It can be stretched to include secular and religious communities. The word family is as imprecise as it is powerful.

This rapid survey of the way we use the word family should flag us a warning as we try to get a grip on what 'Christian family values' may mean. These values are clearly going to vary immensely for different people. What I call my family depends on my life history, my present responsibilities, the people who live in my household and those I relate to and love. My role as a family member is constantly changing. It is certain to be different from yours. Perhaps an important family value for Christians is *recognizing* the variety of families which actually exists.

Grasping how much families vary is vital for the churches. We Christians may hold in our hearts a picture of an ideal family of husband and wife in a lifelong, faithful marriage, together with their children. Unless we realize that such families are more often found on cereal packets than in the estates and streets and villages of this country we are liable to treat most actual families as in some way defective, second-class.

Let us return to Mark's account of Jesus' early ministry. It hardly pictures a son any mother would be proud of. Mark presents a young man who fits into understood categories— itinerant preacher, travelling healer—yet a man his nearest and dearest find puzzling, challenging and exasperating.

Jesus seems to understand the claims his family makes on him. He knows who comprise his family and his expected role within it: he chooses to enlarge the concept to embrace 'anyone who does the will of God'. From now on Jesus will proffer family rights to people totally unrelated to him. With them he will find closeness, intimacy, a sense of belonging.

Late-twentieth-century Christians trying to tease out the concept of family today will not expect to find a ready-made blueprint in Mark's snapshot of Jesus' distressed relatives on the outside and his favoured friends within. But the story remains unsettling: perhaps for Christians family roles are not so clear cut, perhaps it is not so obvious what are 'good' and 'bad' ways of behaving in families. Maybe a person's self-determination or vocation can become more important than his or her family duty. Maybe other imperatives should override the family virtues of niceness and respectability.

Perhaps today's Christian does not inherit family values immutable from the time of Christ. Instead, Mark's Jesus gives us a conflict, a difficulty present since the earliest writing about Christian attitudes to family life. But Christians can also catch there a vigour, an energy, an urgency and enthusiasm to plunge into a new way of living that stretches the bounds of family to an extent hitherto unsuspected.

All this can help us to be more tolerant of people in family set-ups different from our own, and more ready to recognize people whose family cannot attain the ideal. If your own family is up to scratch this means you will have to work on accepting others. If not, you will have to work on accepting yourself as well.

The task is made easier because we know that Jesus preferred the company of the poor and unsuccessful, whom he called the *anawim* or little ones, to hobnobbing with the righteous. Jesus recognized all kinds of people who were not very respectable. If we sit with those the Pharisees despise we shall be in good company.

If Christians can go some way towards *recognizing* the many different types of family, we may be surprised and delighted to discover God at work in the most unlikely places.

Taking stock

The dilemma of Jesus' own family can be used as a way of starting to pray for the Christian family value of *recognizing* the many different kinds of family.

Becoming quiet
Approach the story with still thoughts and a quiet mind.

The grace
Father, help us to rejoice in the variety of families around us. Show us your love working in families of every kind.

The story
Mark's account of Jesus' own family is given at the start of this chapter.

Bringing it home
A crowded house, jam-packed with people. Feel the hot air coming out through the doorway. Sniff the not-too-savoury bodies. Look in through the door. What can you see? Can you make out Jesus at all, or hear him talking somewhere beyond the crush?

Now think about some people you know who admittedly fall short of the Christian family ideal. Maybe you know a divorced

person who left home and family, or an unmarried couple who
live together, or a couple in their second marriage with their
blended family. Think of them by name. Perhaps you could let
them go into the crowded house. Let them sit with the others
in a tightly-packed circle around Jesus.

Outside the house is Jesus' family, and perhaps next to them
a good Christian family. Father and mother, married in church,
loyal and faithful to each other, together with their two well
brought up children. Maybe you could let them stand outside
the house with Jesus' family.

Now put yourself into the picture. Go up to the Christian
family. Look at them. How do you feel? Can you identify with
them? Or do you perhaps feel jealous, or inferior? Talk with this
couple about those inside. Do you pity the insiders at all, and
if so, is your pity tinged with any condescension or disapproval?
Is there any feeling that the family outside is first-class, while
those inside are second-class Christians?

Now go in and listen to what Jesus is saying to the insiders.
Do you feel like sitting down as one of them? What responsi-
bility do you feel for those outside, and for their point of view?
What do you decide to do about it?

Now let the story unroll again in your mind.

Some thoughts for today's families

Maybe 'doing the will of the Father' includes the unconven-
tional and unexpected. Being part of Jesus' new family seems
to include being on familiar terms with a wider range of people
than we could ever have imagined. There could be richness
here.

Perhaps you could talk to Jesus about other people whom
you find hard to accept because of their lifestyles. Leave him to
show you bit by bit how to value them for themselves.

During the next week you might try asking someone who
lives rather differently from you about something that is important to them. See whether you can have any 'family feeling'
with them.

Chapter 3

WHY HAVE YOU DONE THIS?

Families come in many varieties. It is important not to take one type of family as the norm and to marginalize the rest. I accept and delight in the different forms of family. They seem to me a sign of God's exuberance.

The variety among families shows how slippery the concept of family can be. Yet, even if a particular family is defined and its boundaries understood, important questions remain. What is going on in families? How do they work? What makes a family successful? How can I improve the quality of my family's life, or help someone else to improve theirs? Here it must be remembered how much every single family changes with the passage of time. Some analysts distinguish seven successive stages in the course of a family's life: here are my own names for them, and the sort of things which happen in families at each stage.

1. *Free spirits* are an unrelated couple preparing to form a new family. Their tasks in life are to become independent of their parents, to establish themselves in work, and to form and sustain friendships with others like themselves.

2. If such a couple set up home together, and more especially when they marry they may be called *dinkies*, a family with dual income and no kids. Their efforts will go into creating a home, exchanging their independence for interdependence, and learning how to live in closeness and intimacy without feeling overwhelmed. Each may seek to get their partner accepted in their family of origin and to find a place for themselves in their partner's original family.

3. *Young parents* have to learn how to become mother or father as well as lovers, to cope with a small baby, to accept responsibility for a dependent child. They see their own parents transformed into grandparents, their brothers into uncles, their sisters into aunts. As other children arrive, brother and sister relationships are set up, and the original couple have to learn to balance the children's needs and wants against each other's and their own.

4. *Adolescent families* have to cope with several changes at once.

Children demand more freedom yet need boundaries and continuing support. Parents often realign work roles, as mother takes up more outside work and father recognizes career limitations; both parents may hit a mid-life crisis, as they recognize how many earlier ambitions remain unfulfilled. Their own parents may now become dependent and require care.

5. *Empty nesters* have to contend with the independence of their children. They may need to rediscover each other and to learn to live again as a couple. They must relate to their children's partners as they marry, together with these partners' parents and families. The arrival of grandchildren opens up a new way of relating to the young: closeness without ultimate responsibility.

6. *Active oldies* find themselves moving over, letting their children become the 'middle generation' with responsibility for young and old. New opportunities for travel, sports and hobbies, and for political, church and social work can open for those with good health.

7. *Last lappers* have to cope with frailty, ill-health and loss of independence. They have to face the death of their partner and their friends, and ultimately their own death.

This seven-stage life-course way of looking at a family can do much to help us understand what is currently going on in our own family or in families we are trying to help. It clarifies the losses which a family often has to sustain at each stage and the emotional tasks it may have to undertake. It shows the family's need to be resilient in the face of loss. It helps us to ask where power may lie at any given stage or who carries what degree of responsibility.

The seven stages are by no means clear cut or the same for every family. Often they merge and overlap. When a family is passing from one stage to another it is then at its most vulnerable. Here are some case histories, with names changed, which illustrate these transitions.

When Lorraine and Neil first married he seemed to spend every night out with his friends while Lorraine went home to chat with her mother. Lorraine often accepted invitations for them both or took on extra work without letting Neil know. Neil, on the other hand, was far into plans to accept promotion with relocation in a distant town before he consulted Lorraine about it. Resolving these difficulties and learning to trust and confide in each other was a vital part of their transition from *free spirits* to *dinkies*.

Ian and Sandra's first baby settled down quickly and always slept well in the mornings. One Saturday Ian wanted them to go to the DIY store to choose some wallpaper. Sandra did not want to disturb the baby to dress her for the outing, so they popped down to the store without her. On the way home they both imagined the baby dying from fire, intruders or sudden illness and vowed they would never leave her alone in the house again. An important step had been taken in the transition from *dinkies* to trustworthy *young parents*.

Martin came home one Friday looking forward to his two days' rest from work. His wife Debbie reminded him of his promise to cope with the family while she went off on a long-planned study weekend. Their fourteen-year-old daughter burst in asking to stay with a friend the family did not know, while their thirteen-year-old son claimed that he was now old enough to go to a distant football match on his own. Just then the phone rang: it was the neighbour of Debbie's invalid widowed mother saying 'Someone's got to come. I really can't be responsible for her any more.' It is hard to become the 'middle generation' attempting to reconcile all these conflicting interests. It is particularly difficult to trust young people, yet still to be responsible for their welfare. Facing up to such decisions marks the transition from *young parents* to *adolescent families*.

Fiona and Frank were on the first holiday they had spent alone for years. Fiona sent cards to their married children, to their in-laws and to those she called their out-laws, the family of the nice girl their son currently lived with. They tried to decide what to do that afternoon. Frank suggested something their son would have liked, then something their daughter would have enjoyed. 'But what would *we* like, Frank?' said Fiona. Learning to trust and enjoy each other anew is not easy for parents who have lived somewhat through their children. As they pass from *adolescent families* to *empty nesters* the losses of parents are obvious. The gains have yet to be discovered.

James and Shirley enjoyed meeting their granddaughter Sophie from school and looking after her until her mother returned from work. They did not really mind missing the afternoon bowls matches for Sophie, but went in the evenings instead. However, when the bowls club arranged a tour of Australia and New Zealand, James found himself telling his daughter that she would have to make other arrangements for Sophie for two months while they were away. *Empty nesters* who can trust their family to run quite successfully without them make the easiest transition to *active oldies*.

Phyllis had very severe arthritis but her husband Sid helped her to dress and do her hair beautifully. Phyllis wrote shopping lists and Sid did the shopping. She managed to cook their meals as long as he lifted the heavy pans and washed up. One day Sid suffered a sudden heart attack and died before the ambulance arrived at hospital. After the funeral their middle-aged children asked Phyllis how she was going to manage now. *Active oldies* have to come to terms with the loss of health, independence and life itself as they face up to the *last lap*. No gain is apparent here. Only the Christian trust in the resurrection points to a gain 'that no eye has seen and no ear has heard, things beyond the mind of man, all that God has prepared for those who love him' (1 Corinthians 2).

The life-course scheme helps to explain what is happening in the family as time passes from the point of view of one couple. It tries to show the impact on all family members at each stage but avoids impossible complexity by assuming the key couple's viewpoint. From this point of view a man may become independent of his mother at stage 1, receive her into his home as a dependant at stage 4, and may himself become dependent on his children at stage 7. At each stage the key couple accepts loss, takes on new tasks, and negotiates change with other family members. Successful family life at any stage depends upon the family's ability to cope with change. Yet even a successful stage will eventually crumble and the family must then perforce face up to the work of the next.

Unfinished business from one stage can resurface to complicate another. Karen went straight from her parents' home into marriage at stage 2, without first establishing herself independently in stage 1. She made a strong bid for independence at stage 4 by taking on a demanding full-time job. When this was threatened by the need to care for her sick father Karen's inward rage was intense. When her father came to live with them Karen had to take part-time work. She became deeply depressed and had to stop working altogether.

Some couples find their experience straddles several stages. Children born to elderly parents, couples who marry very young or very late in life or at widely different ages, those who have children late in a marriage or who have a later baby when their first children are teenagers, those who remarry and start a second family—all these can find themselves tackling tasks from several stages at once. Paul and Sheila felt out of step with the other parents as they sat on low chairs watching their son act Joseph in the infants' nativity play. 'Who would believe that last week we became grandparents?' whispered Paul. Such experiences should warn against thinking of the life-course as inevitably composed of compulsory stages which must all be encountered in a given order. A family's course varies with individual families, regions and cultures. Where families run a different course from the majority of those around them they may need extra flexibility in the face of change.

The idea of a family's life-course shows that even the most regular families, the families where 'nothing ever happens', have change built into them. One answer to the question at the start of this chapter—What is going on in families? How do they work?—is that families pass from stage to stage, they take the inevitable losses and they enjoy the attendant gains. What makes a family successful is its ability to cope with inevitable change.

During the transition from one stage to the next a family often feels lost and uncertain. For instance, a couple with a new baby may feel awkward. Their customary confidence deserts them. Their ability to predict each other's actions disappears. They feel inferior to more practised parents. They may suspect that others are criticizing them. Alternatively, they may meet nothing but kindness from experienced parents who remember how they felt with their first baby, and may gain a sense of solidarity with other new parents who are also learning the routines of feeding, sleeping and nappy changing. Feelings of loss and uncertainty may equally hit a newly retired couple, who miss their work and its sense of purpose and who may find other active oldies impossibly self-motivated and organized.

Not all change is of the life-course, evolutionary type. Families are always vulnerable to tragedy. Unemployment, homelessness and poverty may be undeserved and unlooked for. Nobody volunteers for disability, illness, accident and sudden death, which can strike at any stage and can confound every expectation. All require a radical readjustment, giving up what might have been and accepting what is. Family members may help each other to bear trouble, but whenever one receives a blow of fate a knock-on effect may be suffered by all the others. Families which experience these thunderbolts may feel unlucky or cursed, singled out for punishment. 'Why did it happen to us?' cry parents whose child is disabled. 'Why did God allow it?' Their grief is compounded by others who, in their guilt at having perfect children, give them pitying glances or cross the road as they approach.

A happier type of change is one that is freely chosen. A planned house move, a deliberate career choice, a longed-for pregnancy can be welcomed far more positively than when these are unwillingly accepted. The family sees something is good and goes for it, although even chosen change brings inevitable losses of familiar friends or freedoms. Such choices may make a family feel powerful, capable or brave, but they may find others seem jealous of their good fortune. Sometimes they lose friends who appear weaker than themselves, sometimes they gain others who admire their success.

Yet another type of change comes as a result of wrongdoing or foolishness, as when family members lose their licence for drunk driving or contract lung cancer through smoking 50 cigarettes a day. Drink, drugs, sexual adventures, brushes with the law, all can cause family disruption and family grief. Families may react to such changes with remorse and recrimination, or they may grit their teeth and accept the situation stoically. Often they have to contend with lack of sympathy from outsiders, who righteously distance themselves from such self-inflicted woes.

There is a family change which I hold to be of a different order from all others. This is the change of marriage breakdown. Much more will be said of this in later chapters but here it is interesting to see how marital breakdown can share something of all the other sorts of family change. A couple once suited seem to grow apart, to step out of a stage that unified them into one where they have nothing in common. Often their breakup seems to come out of the blue, yet with hindsight it appears inevitable. One or other partner can exercise choices that seem utterly selfish yet at the same time they may feel driven or at their wits' end or at the mercy of fate. To outsiders their wounds may seem self-inflicted or richly deserved; to the couple each feels the victim of intolerable lack of understanding or of cruel and hateful betrayal. No wonder that their own emotions are so confused and the attitudes of others towards them so unpredictable. The different kinds of change which families experience are summarized in the table below.

Some types of change affecting families

Change	Dominant feature	We may feel	Others may seem
Life course	inevitable	lost inferior	superior supportive
Bolt from the blue	accidental	unlucky cursed singled out	guilty pitying avoiding
Free choice	elective	powerful brave capable	jealous admiring weak
Just deserts	consequential	remorseful stoical	self-righteous unsympathetic
Marital breakdown	all the above	all the above	all the above

It is clear that ability to cope with change is the hallmark of a successful family. A great deal is now known about the way we deal with change. The stages many people go through can be charted on what is called a transition curve, reproduced pictorially in the figure on p. 22. This curve has its high points and low points. Not everybody goes through all the stages, but the stages usually come in the same order.

These are the stages the transition curve illustrates:

1: **Denial** Sometimes it is hard to accept that a change is really happening. We feel numb. We need to go over events again and again in our mind before we know that the change really did occur.

2: **Elation** This happens when we see only the gains and lose sight of the losses. We are full of plans for the future. Or, we take a loss unnaturally well, so that people say 'Isn't he brave?' or 'Isn't she marvellous?'. At such times God can seem very close.

3: **Searching** As the elation wears off we can find ourselves unsure, lacking in confidence. Sometimes we revisit places where we don't

The transition curve

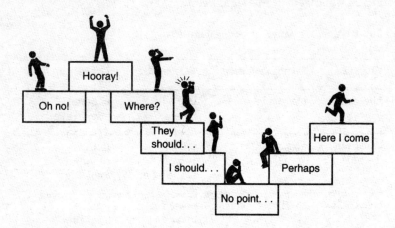

belong any more. Sometimes we wonder where God is, or whether God really exists.

4: **Anger** As we realize just what we have lost we may feel very angry. We may hate or blame other people. Often we feel like hating or blaming God.

5: **Guilt** Another common feeling is that it's all our fault. We feel if only we'd acted differently things would have turned out better. We can feel as though God is punishing us.

6: **Depression** This is the lowest point. Nothing seems worthwhile. All joy in life has gone and even God seems far away.

7: **Acceptance** Bit by bit we stop dwelling on what we have lost. Occasionally we catch ourselves feeling happy again. We can make a few plans for the future. We may start to ask God for things again, to make small bargains with God.

8: **Resumption of life** Now we're back in our stride. Losses are accepted. Gains are enjoyed. We can say Amen and go forward trusting in God.

The transition process is the same for trivial matters like missing the bus or losing a credit card as it is for tragedies like major illness, marriage breakdown or the death of a close relative. In small losses the whole transition can be over in seconds; in serious bereavement it can take years.

In big changes, trying to move straight from *Hooray!* to *Here I come* is like walking a tightrope—very precarious and easy to fall off. Most people have first to live through the other stages in turn. Trying to 'pull yourself together' doesn't really work. Taking time to work through each stage in turn is not self-indulgent but helps a person finally to recover successfully.

This whole chapter has been about change. Two questions asked at the beginning have still to be faced: How can I improve the quality of my family's life? How can I help someone else to improve theirs? One important way of doing this is to be with your own or other families as they go through the transition curve and undergo change.

It is helpful, though not essential, if you have experienced the type of change other people are facing: being in the same boat brings a solidarity which makes it easier to be open. It is best to avoid advice or expecting them to cope like you. Listen to what they say and help them to talk about what is happening and how they feel about it. Let them go over the same ground as often as they want to. It helps to try and see where they are on the transition curve. The aim is not to jolly them along, but to stay with them where they are until they are ready to move on.

At times of family change you can lose all certainty. Habits are no longer effective. Familiar ways of coping no longer seem to work. For the time being you feel lost, adrift, out of control. Then the greatest asset can be a trusting nature. You may have to risk telling others how you feel and what your difficulties are. You may have to trust them to show you how to adapt to your new situation.

If you are trying to help someone else through a period of change you will have to trust them to make progress at their own pace, and not insist on instant solutions. Staying with others as they cope with change is a real expression of Christian charity, especially when their troubles seem self-inflicted or undeserving of help. Showing that you trust and believe in them may be an important ingredient in their success.

Trust is the Christian family value most needed in times of change. It is not a naive guarantee that nothing will go wrong. Rather it is a trust that God never deserts his children and loves them to the end.

Taking stock

Becoming quiet
Approach the story with stilled thoughts and a quiet mind.

The grace
Father, it is easy for families to lose their bearings at times of change. Help us to go forward placing all our trust in you.

The story

Every year his parents used to go to Jerusalem for the feast of the Passover. When he was twelve years old, they went up for the feast as usual. When they were on their way home after the feast, the boy Jesus stayed behind in Jerusalem without his parents knowing it.

They assumed he was with the caravan, and it was only after a day's journey that they went to look for him among their relations and acquaintances. When they failed to find him they went back to Jerusalem looking for him everywhere.

Three days later, they found him in the Temple, sitting among the doctors, listening to them, and asking them questions; and all those who heard him were astounded at his intelligence and his replies.

They were overcome when they saw him, and his mother said to him, 'My child, why have you done this to us? See how worried your father and I have been, looking for you.'

'Why were you looking for me?' he replied. 'Did you not know that I must be busy with my Father's affairs?' But they did not understand what he meant.

He then went down with them and came to Nazareth and lived under their authority.

Luke 2

Bringing it home
Imagine the camp, a day's journey from Jerusalem. See the sun go down. Feel the air getting chilly. Sniff the smoke from the camp fires, and the smell of supper cooking. Notice a flurry of activity as the women become more and more agitated. See the men join in and rush around. Hear the cry go up, as people frantically call and shout through the camp for twelve-year-old Jesus. Now put yourself in the picture. Are you Mary, or Joseph,

or one of their family or friends? How do you feel as time goes on and Jesus is still missing? Feel the despondency as people stop looking and all is quiet. Realize that Jesus must be in Jerusalem, in who knows what company.

Now imagine the scene in the Temple. Is it hot and stuffy or cool and shady? Is it empty or full of people? What about the sounds? The smells? Can you make out that little group of men sitting by the pillar? Hear the murmur of their voices. Put yourself into this picture. Are you Mary, or Joseph, or a bystander? Perhaps you are one of the learned men around Jesus. As the scene unfolds, sense the amazement of the doctors: how do they react to this distraught woman interrupting their discourse with the interesting boy? Feel his parents' mixture of anxiety, relief and reproach.

Watch Jesus as he recognizes his parents. Hear him reply to them, and see him go with them into the sun outside.

Go over the story again, notice how you feel, watch Jesus and then talk to him about your experience.

Some thoughts for today's families

Luke's story is set at a time of transition for Jesus' family. Before his twelfth birthday he was considered a child. After his birthday and Bar Mitzvah he belonged with the men and started to assume adult responsibilities. It seems that neither he nor his parents knew quite how to cope with the transition. Only after the grief and pain of getting it wrong could they begin to see how to get it right.

'They did not understand.' Our children are not ourselves. Is it inevitable that parents can never fully understand their children?

In loss and uncertainty we can either despair or 'hope against hope'. Maybe you could develop a habit of trust in God when times of uncertainty come.

Chapter 4
THE WINE RUNS OUT

Families take varied courses. Their members grow and change, they make different choices, fate deals with them differently. Analysing seven stages in the course of a family's life helps me to look at what may be happening in that family but never sets limits on the way families ought to behave. Families show the warmth and depth of their love in ways that defy analysis.

Many families take the form that they do and behave as they do in response to a broken marriage. In many ways this is the greatest misfortune that can affect a family. Love dies, hopes are shattered, expectations are dashed, and yet families re-form and do their best to care. Once marriage breakdown is a fact the survivors deserve every help and respect for their efforts to make a success of family life.

There is a story of two swimmers standing on the bank of a fast-flowing river. Floating downstream came men, women and children, half-drowned and shouting for help. Both swimmers rescued as many as they could. Then one walked off. 'Where are you going?' called the other. 'Stay and help me get them out!' 'No', replied the first. 'I'm going upstream to see what's making them fall in.'

Going upstream from family distress I come to marriage breakdown. The fact that many families cope, and cope admirably, after marriage breakdown does not minimize its traumatic impact on the family. I maintain that the breakdown of marriage poses the greatest single threat to the welfare and happiness of families today. Families are wounded by broken marriage as by nothing else.

Any book entitled *Making Families Work* must try to understand what is happening to marriage. How did we arrive at this situation? Why do people find it so hard to stay married now? Is divorce the only answer to marital conflict? What changes could help marriages survive and grow strong? Can the Christian churches, with their ideals about faithful and lifelong marriage, make any difference?

No book about families can dodge these questions. Strong marriages hold couples together, but they also hold families together. Marriage breakdown strikes at the family's very heart. When marriages fail families are wounded and are liable to disintegrate. The central part of this book about families looks squarely at the chances of saving families by saving marriage.

For most of my adult life I have worked for the Catholic Marriage Advisory Council (CMAC), first as a voluntary group-worker and then for fifteen years as a paid worker at their headquarters. CMAC is an organization of Roman Catholics who work for marriage and family life. In spite of inheriting a rather authoritarian title CMAC is a genuine counselling organization; in fact it is the largest group of Christian counsellors in the United Kingdom, with some 500 trained counsellors working from 80 or so centres.

Counselling is about listening to clients, offering them warmth, acceptance, respect and understanding. It helps them to explore the thoughts and feelings they have about their life and the values they hold, so that they can choose appropriate action. It takes them through a process of problem-solving but always leaves them in control of their own decisions. For nearly half a century CMAC has listened to people whose family life is under stress.

It is not easy to maintain a counselling attitude when you work within a church renowned for its rules and regulations. The very title 'Catholic' suggests to many that they will be judged, shown where they went wrong and told what to do next. So everyone working with CMAC learns to be clear about their own principles but never to impose these on others.

CMAC counsellors believe and declare that marriage is meant to be faithful and lifelong. Yet they understand and accept it when, after every effort at reconciliation, a particular couple recognize that their relationship has died and cannot be revived. Inevitably there is a tension here which all the Christian churches experience; those working with CMAC perhaps feel it as keenly as any.

Can this tension be resolved at all? Marriage is the cement which holds families together and if Christians are concerned for the family they will want marriages to last. Maybe we can understand and face up to marriage breakdown better if we look at the changes affecting marriage in recent times.

Peter and I married halfway through the 1950s. If anyone had asked us why we were marrying, we should have said we were in love. The decision to marry followed on from expectations which we had probably internalized from our families and our church. Others pushed us in the same direction: our friends, neighbours and employers, and that combination of the institutionalized, respectable and successful which later came to be called 'the establishment'.

We had no quarrel with the idea of marrying: we wanted to make public the decision we had come to privately that we belonged together and wanted to live together. When we had sexual intercourse we wanted to have made a home for any possible children, for contraception was not then very reliable and in any case it was forbidden by our church. We thought of our marriage as a contract; it was a contract that we made freely but which then somehow took on a life of its own and was not within our power to break. This conviction we got from our church and I think we found it a source of strength. Our own hesitations and reservations were made resolute and, as people said in those days, we took the plunge.

As married people we had fairly clear roles. Peter was the breadwinner, which included working long hours and on Saturdays. I worked until we had our first child and we found that my wages 'helped', but we thought of my main work as keeping house. Without benefit of washing machine or dishwasher, without refrigerator, freezer or microwave, without plastics or easy-care synthetic fabrics this seemed to be fairly arduous and time-consuming, and I was glad when Peter 'helped' me with some of the chores.

Our marriage was perhaps typical of marriage viewed as an institution, as something already 'there', fixed and definite, with clear expectations and roles. Couples expressed their love and commitment by entering this state, taking on these roles, and trying to fulfil them successfully. Ours was among the last of such marriages, for the 1960s were soon upon us. Throughout the next two decades I kept in close touch with the aspirations of couples getting married by running numerous marriage preparation courses in the name of CMAC.

The 1960s in this country was a time of full employment and prosperity. At last labour-saving gadgets relieved the round of household drudgery, and also removed the need for skill so that chores could be done by everybody. At last wages rose and working hours shortened, and people had leisure to think how to please themselves and money to spend doing it. The grip of the establishment loosened. Young people no longer stepped from school into the adult world, they now had their own culture. Whether used inside or outside of marriage, the contraceptive pill offered a prospect of reliable fertility control. The whole of society seemed transformed. If old institutions were to be retained they would have to be redefined.

Marriage was now spoken of as a personal commitment. Berger and Kellner wrote in 1964 of marriage as 'a dramatic act in which two strangers come together and redefine themselves', saying that its dominant themes were 'romantic love, sexual fulfilment, self-discovery and self-realization through love and sexuality'. The 1969 Divorce Reform Act did away with the concepts of 'innocent' and 'guilty' parties and made the sole ground for granting a divorce the fact that a marriage relationship had irretrievably broken down. Marriage was becoming a more private arrangement.

In time the Christian churches came to recognize this more personal way of looking at marriage, so that the Second Vatican Council of the Roman Catholic church defined marriage as 'a community of life and love' and the Church of England described it as 'a relational bond of personal love'. Defining marriage personally rather than as an institution tends to raise the stakes. If your relationship is rewarding it encourages you and helps deepen your commitment, if your relationship is lacking it depresses you and causes you to look for a way out. Divorce rates climbed steadily throughout the 1960s.

The 1970s saw men's and women's roles revalued both at work and in the home. Married women asked why in this community of life and love it was still they who washed their husband's smelly socks. One newly-married girl told me that she did not even mind doing that: 'It's picking them up from the floor where he's dropped them that I find demeaning.' I puzzled about this afterwards, since I had often picked up Peter's socks and not minded too much: I reasoned that he, too, had coped with some pretty unpleasant tasks during our marriage, like disposing of the afterbirth when our children were born at home or emptying the chemical toilet on our canal boat holidays.

Gradually my consciousness of the unequal life chances of men and women was raised, and I learned from people like Jessie Bernard, writing in 1973, that there can be two marriages in every partnership. 'His' marriage may be quite satisfactory, offering him a comfortable haven from the world of work, while 'her' marriage can carry most of the burden of domestic work and childcare and deprive her of friends and a career outside the home.

Arguments about roles in marriage continued throughout the 1970s; they were not so much about the tasks in themselves but about the underlying lack of respect and equality that such tasks symbolized. Some women were able to negotiate changes, some continued to pick up their husband's socks, but more and more found they could not tolerate that and similar assaults on their new sense of self-worth. Divorce rates continued to rise throughout the 1970s.

By the 1980s equality in marriage was exposed as more notional than real. An ongoing study by One Plus One of 65 couples who had married in 1979 showed that, whereas many couples maintained that household chores were shared equally, in fact they were mostly done by the wives. The chores themselves may not have put much strain on these marriages, the 'frustration of expectations' undoubtedly did.

The 1980s saw other contradictions. Unemployment rose side by side with the suddenly affluent enterprise culture, more people claimed benefits at the same time as they were newly blamed for not functioning without help, house prices started a long fall just after unprecedented numbers had borrowed unprecedented sums to be able to buy.

Although marriage is largely seen today as a personal and almost private commitment, social and economic pressures do affect married relationships: divorce rates are lowest among the professional classes, are four times higher among unskilled manual workers and are highest of all among unemployed people whatever their social class. It looks as though couples who married to enhance their lives found the disappointing reality more than they could bear.

There is a dark side to the private world of marriage. One in eight crimes of violence happens in the home and one in four women suffer domestic violence at some time. The law now recognizes the crime of marital rape. We are now more aware of the physical and sexual abuse of children. Infidelity, drunkenness, meanness and fecklessness have always put a strain on marriages. Such miseries might be tolerated for the sake of a marriage contract; once marriage is seen as a community of life and love they become intolerable and divorce seems inevitable.

Rising divorce rates are common throughout the Western world; in this country they have increased sixfold during the lifetime of my own marriage. Divorced people are no longer unusual, they are a feature of our social life. Disillusion with marriage is widespread: the age of first marriage is later, cohabitation is increasing and fewer couples who live together are marrying when they have children. Most divorced people remarry, as though hoping it was not marriage which failed them but the person they were married to, but second marriages fail even more frequently than first ones.

Research shows that divorce is bad for a couple's health and wretched for their children. Housing, welfare and social services all feel the strain. Worries are voiced that mass divorce, by breaking up families, is threatening the very cohesion of society.

Studies show that regular church goers are less ready to divorce than others: where our daily values equate with our Sunday values our marriages seem more able to survive. Yet those who call themselves Christians are not exempt from mass divorce. We preach that marriage is meant to be faithful and lifelong; we divorce almost as frequently as the rest of our society. It is as though the bride and groom at Cana have brought wine to their wedding symbolizing all their dreams and aspirations. And the wine has failed. The couple know it. The waiters realize, then the steward, and one by one the guests. All of them, all of us stand helpless as the precious wine of love and commitment runs out and is lost in the dry sands of divorce. How can we face up to what is happening? How could the situation possibly be transformed?

One of the foremost thinkers on marriage today is Jack Dominian, former consultant psychiatrist and founder of the Marriage Research Centre, which is now named One Plus One. Dr Dominian is aware of the darker side of marriage and draws attention to the way Christians traditionally cope when things go wrong. Then Christianity calls the wronged partner to high Christian virtues: to forgiveness, to unselfishness, to self-sacrifice, to putting up with trials and difficulties, to carrying one's cross. In the past such virtues were often enough to save a marriage.

Dr Dominian points out how marriage has been raised in Christian thinking. He quotes a recent church law describing marriage as a 'covenant, by which a man and a woman establish between themselves a partnership of their whole life, and which of its own very nature is ordered to the well-being of the spouses'. Such an ideal implies that serious wrongs from one partner to the other are not to be tolerated. It calls Christians to forgiveness, but it then calls the wronged partner beyond forgiveness to something more.

> Clearly it takes time for the spouse to appreciate that a persistent problem exists which appears recurrent and unchangeable. When that moment of realization has arrived, when something fundamental is missing or is wrong with the relationship, what should the spouse do? This is the moment of truth. Everything should be done to challenge the partner about the issue.

This challenge should be very active, Jack Dominian tells couples. Face your partner repeatedly. Ask them to change. Insist that the problem is tackled. Persist, persevere, never let up. Bring in outside help. Only then consider carefully whether you are prepared to lower your expectations and stay, or make up your mind to go. If Dr Dominian is right, marriage calls Christians to go beyond forgiveness, to face up to what is happening and how each has contributed, to confront their problems and to build their partnership anew.

Most people at present feel such a challenge is beyond them.

> What usually happens is that spouses remain frustrated and dissatisfied for years without taking decisive action to confront their partner. Then one day they simply pack their bags and go ...

says Jack Dominian. If renewed partnerships are to replace today's divorces the Christian churches must with all seriousness take on a new role. We have it in our power to help married couples to answer this call for challenge and reconstruction. But first we need to admit that things are in a mess.

We need to stare the mess in the face. We need to face up to the hurt broken relationships cause. We need to recognize that the clock cannot be put back, the genie cannot be forced back into the bottle, we cannot paper over the cracks of failing marriages by asking people to put up with what is intolerable. We need to resist all temptation to apathy or despair. We need to turn to God, our Father, and see what he would have us do. I should like to nominate *realism* in facing the cost of broken marriages as our next Christian family value.

Taking stock

If you would like to pray about *realism* in facing the cost of broken marriages, you could use Jesus' parable of the merciful father.

Becoming quiet

Allow your thoughts to become still and your body to relax.

The grace

Father, help us to face reality. Help us to admit how much broken marriages wound families. Show us what you would have us do about it.

The story

A man had two sons. The younger said to his father, 'Father, let me have the share of the estate that would come to me'. So the father divided the property between them. A few days later, the younger son got together everything he had and left for a distant country where he squandered his money on a life of debauchery.

When he had spent it all, that country experienced a severe famine, and now he began to feel the pinch; so he hired himself out to one of the local inhabitants who put him on his farm to feed the pigs. And he would willingly have filled his belly with the husks the pigs were eating but no one offered him anything.

Then he came to his senses and said, 'How many of my father's paid servants have more food than they want, and here am I dying of hunger! I will leave this place and go to my father and say: Father, I have sinned against heaven and against you; I no longer deserve to be called your son; treat me as one of your paid servants.'

So he left the place and went back to his father.

Luke 15

Bringing it home

Picture the prodigal sitting among the pigs. Watch them rooting for food in the bare earth. Hear them grunt and snort. Feel the sun blazing down.

Then perhaps you could be the prodigal. Feel starvation

gnawing at your stomach. Look at your filthy rags. Maybe shudder as those unclean animals, the pigs, brush against you. Remember how you set out with such high hopes, and feel the disappointment. Think of your father's farm which you might have inherited, and feel the contrast with your life now. Perhaps you struggle with your pride, which does not want to admit how low you have sunk. Then maybe you go beyond pride into total disillusion. Touch the despair. Then think of your father . . .

Stop the story there and run through it again in your mind. As it happens, notice how you feel. When the action is over have a conversation with Jesus, the storyteller. Tell him what you experienced, ask him anything you want, hear what Jesus says to you.

Some thoughts for today's families

Think of a marriage that has broken down: it may be your own, it may be that of someone you love. Think of all the high hopes at the beginning of the marriage, photographs of good times, expectations of being loved and cherished, happy and successful. Look squarely at the ruins of those hopes, the hurt, the disappointment. Admit what has been lost. Take this to God, your Father. Lay it in his lap. Tell him how much you mind.

Think of some ways mass divorce affects society: the damage to children, the effect on health and well-being, the pressure on housing and welfare and grant giving services. Turn to God, the Father of us all. Admit that we are in a mess, that we are finding it impossible as a society to live in love. Ask him to show you in time what you can do to help.

Chapter 5

THEY HAVE NO WINE

Can anything be done to ease the toll which broken marriages are taking on couples and on their families? How should we begin? Mary, the mother of Jesus, shows us the way. Servants, steward, guests, bridegroom and bride, all may have come to realize that something serious was amiss at Cana. Yet transformation could not begin until Mary had the courage to face up to the truth and come out with it: 'They have no wine.'

I once went to an evening class in hostess cookery where the teacher demonstrated an iced walnut sponge. This was intended to be a light, high cake with white icing decorated with walnuts and I do not know why the cake turned out like a flat shortbread. Not a word was said about this disaster. The poor, flat thing was decorated with panache as though it were of imposing height and the cake was presented to us as though it were a great success. Nobody said anything, but none of the students was fooled.

It is easy for couples getting married today to do something similar. Both the secular and the religious world contribute to their high hopes. The behavioural sciences encourage them to look for a partnership of equals in which they will feel respected, cherished and understood. The churches teach them that marriage is a community of life and love. They shrug off small problems easily. Then one day one of them meets a real pinch.

What I am calling a pinch is a situation where one partner feels seriously at odds with the other. Pinches in marriage are inevitable. They may arise because the partnership is between two different people: he likes doing crosswords, she likes visiting museums. They may arise because the partnership is between a man and a woman: he finds it hard to express his feelings, she expects more signs of affection. They may come from differing family customs: his mother made the early morning tea whereas her father usually did.

Pinches may arise because one is tight or free with money,

one is sexually cold or very demanding, one is quick-tempered or shows no feeling, one is keener than the other on hobbies or visiting family or going to church. Pinches in themselves do not mean that the marriage is going wrong. They are a sign that the marriage is ready for further growth.

What often happens next is that the pinch frightens the wife or husband who experiences it. They expect their marriage to be rewarding. When the reality seems otherwise they cannot really believe it. They see their partner acting as though nothing is wrong, nothing important is at stake.

They have been told that marriage must be worked at, so they set to and dress up the reality. They make it look as much like their expectation as possible, just as the demonstrator ignored the flat cake and proceeded to decorate it as if nothing were amiss. In their hearts they know the marriage fails to meet their expectations, but still they keep on trying until eventually they run out of steam. Months or years or even decades later they 'simply pack their bags and go'.

Mary the mother of Jesus shows a better way, the way of facing up to reality and speaking with confidence to the person you love. It is a way of courage, a way of risk. It is a way of taking up the cross, not by silent suffering but by taking up the issue. It is a way recommended by Jesus:

> If your brother does something wrong, go and have it out with
> him alone, between your two selves. If he listens to you, you have
> won back your brother.
>
> Matthew 18

A pinch may be felt by either partner. An example might be that Jan and Trevor agreed that Jan should give up her bank account when she stopped work to have their first baby. They both thought it would save bank charges to have just one account which Trevor would manage. In the event Jan finds Trevor extremely mean in the way he handles this account, while he thinks the money is much better managed than before.

Taking up a pinch like this is often called confrontation, and this is the term used by those who teach the skills of relating. In their jargon it does not mean to attack or to be aggressive or combative. Rather, the term confrontation is used to mean bringing a pinch 'up front', having the courage to face up to it and to put it before the person who caused it.

The process of confrontation has been analysed in great detail.

It is taught to business men and women, who can use it to win boardroom battles or to outdo employees. I think success in marriage is more important and more difficult than business success. I believe that skills often used in business to manipulate and exploit can be used by married people in all honesty, truth and love. I should like to take the example of Jan and Trevor to illustrate the process of confronting someone you disagree with.

At first Jan ignores the problem. It is trivial, she thinks, not worth making a fuss about. Let it pass. But her irritation persists and does not improve with time. In fact she becomes more resentful each time she has to ask Trevor for money. She begins to dislike Trevor for his meanness.

Jan wonders if she should say something to Trevor but is afraid of being a moaner. What Jesus says is that problems between people must be faced with courage. A problem is not a complaint. A difficulty is not a complaint. Jan's feelings are Jan's feelings, and if she thinks something is wrong between her and Trevor she should say so. Jesus puts the onus for this on to the person feeling the pinch: 'If your brother does something wrong, go and have it out with him.'

Still Jan hesitates. Perhaps she should keep quiet for the sake of peace. But what kind of peace is that? Jan still feels Trevor is treating her unfairly. Peace without justice is a false peace, a 'peace and quiet' which papers over the cracks, a game of Happy Christian Families which can lead eventually to the marriage breaking down. Jesus says that the initiative for change must come from the partner who is wronged or who recognizes that something in the relationship is not acceptable. Go, says Jesus, and have it out. Summon your courage. Risk conflict, risk challenge, risk confrontation, or you will never find the real peace that is based on truth and justice.

How should Jan make the challenge? What is the right way to confront someone? Jesus makes it clear why Jan is doing this. She wants Trevor to listen. This won't happen if she dumps her problems on an unaware partner and expects them to be sorted out there and then. Far better to say something like 'It's not working, is it? When can we sort it out?' or 'I'm not happy. Can we fix a time to talk?'

When the time comes it won't help if Jan goes in with all guns blazing. It won't help to blame, shame or attack. Her aim is to get Trevor to listen and he can't do that if he is defending himself. A better way is for Jan to find something in Trevor's handling of money that does please her, to affirm before she confronts. Something like 'I'm really relieved that we've got no worries about unpaid bills. Thank you for being so reliable at paying them.' Jan's affirmation of Trevor should be heartfelt and truthful. This is not manipulation. This is not soft soap. This is a genuinely loving wife finding common ground with her lover.

Next Jan states her problem. And that is how she states it, as her problem. Not 'You're mean. Tight-fisted. A Scrooge. A skin-flint.' But 'I'm not happy about the money. Can you help?' It is best if Jan can focus on a particular example and say how she felt. 'When I had to ask you for money for that skirt I felt like a child asking for more pocket money.'

A period of clarification follows. The hope is that Trevor will listen to Jan. Since he was unaware of Jan's pinch he will need to ask for more information. How long has she felt like this? What has changed since they agreed on one bank account? What makes the arrangement easier or harder to bear? Is it the way he handles money or his attitude to her that upsets Jan? He may need to look at his behaviour through Jan's eyes and ask himself some questions. Does he really think of her as a child now that she spends her time at home with the baby? Has he slipped into his father's way of doing things without remembering that times have changed and Jan is a very different person from his mother?

Even before they look for a solution Jan will find that her problem eases just by being understood. It is hard to have a problem, but the hurt is doubled when it is inflicted by an apparently uncaring, callous person who out of the whole world is supposed to be your best friend and lover. If Trevor can listen, can hear what Jan is saying and understand what she is feeling, can say 'I had no idea you felt like that. You deserve better from me', then his reasons and justifications are easier to hear because her hurt is already soothed.

Ideally this period of clarification continues until both can say something like 'The way we handle money does not suit us any more. It does not reflect our sense of equality or our esteem for each other.' The problem is now a joint problem. Once it changes from one person's pinch to a shared pinch couples are usually very creative in finding a solution that uniquely suits themselves.

There is no single right solution to Jan and Trevor's problem. Any way they choose to handle their money is good as long as they both agree and their bills are met. Good solutions to problems, the WIN/WIN solutions, allow both parties to gain something: Jan gains a sense that she still functions as a respected adult while Trevor gains peace of mind about their bills. The best solutions specify what action should be taken, and choose action that can be achieved and measured and which actually solves the problem.

Now comes the good part. Jan's pinch is probably solved. Both she and Trevor gain a sense of common purpose in carrying out the new regime. But their gain is much greater than that. Confronting pinches deepens understanding. Jan and Trevor explore the meaning money holds for each of them. This understanding stays with them and makes their marriage stronger. What was once a problem now becomes a strength. This is so for any pinch, whatever the cause and whether it is first felt by a wife or by a husband. Successful confrontation deepens commitment. In their own lives husbands and wives see the words of Jesus coming true: 'If he listens to you, you have won back your brother.'

The process of successful confrontation can be summarized like this:

1. One partner feels a pinch. The other is oblivious.

2. The partner feeling the pinch decides the matter is not trivial and will not go away.

3. The partner feeling the pinch resolves to confront the other.

4. A time is set.

5. The confrontation is made in the form: 'When you ... I feel ... because ...'

6. The other listens and asks for clarification.

7. Discussion continues until the problem is understood and shared.

8. A WIN/WIN solution is agreed which is achievable, behavioural, measurable and worthwhile.

9. The couple co-operate in the new solution.

10. The confrontation results in deeper commitment.

Some couples solve pinches almost instinctively and do not

need the process elaborated. Most couples get stuck at some time, and then it is helpful to see at which stage the hold-up occurs. Is it because the person feeling the pinch ignores it? Is it because they lack courage and dare not confront their partner? Is it because they spring the problem on an unsuspecting partner, or try to shame or blame them into compliance. Is it because they want to change their partner and to get their own way rather than to seek listening and understanding? Is it because a wife or a husband doesn't listen to their partner's troubles? Is it because they try for a quick fix before they reach a common understanding? Is it because they set unrealistic goals?

Business men and women can use confrontation skills for short-term commercial gain. Married people have much more at stake. They are working at a lifelong, loving relationship. If they have courage to take up pinches they can become skilled experts in the art of successful confrontation.

Every time a couple solve a problem together they gain in understanding and commitment. That is how relationships are formed. By the time a couple marry they will have been hundreds of times round the cycle of commitment–pinch–confrontation–understanding–solution–deeper commitment. That is how relationships grow. If their marriage is to continue they must have the courage to go round this cycle hundreds more times. They must become so skilled at this cycle that their relationship can stand up to all the pressures pulling them apart.

Conflict in marriage is inevitable. This is especially so in times of change, and the changes in our own times are unprecedented and ever accelerating. The chief changes affecting families have already been analysed in Chapter 3, and all can cause conflict between married couples. Couples expect some changes as they set up home, have children, bring them up, see the children leave, embrace active retirement and support each other in old age. They must also adjust to changes in their expectations from such blows as business failure, unemployment or redundancy, from infertility, ill health, disability or sudden death. There are free choices which nevertheless require both husband and wife to be adaptable, such as moving work or home, taking promotion or going for early retirement. Sometimes couples have to adapt to the consequences of unwise choices, and must cope with the loss of home, job, health or freedom. And lastly there are changes within the partners, as each learns more, follows new ideas, finds new interests, discovers hidden talents and responds to the changing times.

All these changes require the couple to take up pinches with courage. Life expectancy is greater today than ever before. A couple marrying in their twenties may expect to be alive in their eighties and beyond. Bringing up today's small families takes fewer of those years than formerly. For the rest they will stay together only if they grow together rather than grow apart. For this they need the skill to resolve conflict in a way that continually deepens their commitment.

It is my belief that young men and women enter marriage today with the hope and determination to succeed. They do not want their marriage to fail. If they are shown the vital skill of resolving conflict I think they will be keen to try it. They will experience the warmth and strength of 'winning back their brother'. Before they marry they could become practised at taking up pinches and solving them together. They could discover that resolving conflict needs time and patience and being open to change. They could realize that committing themselves to marriage commits them to use this skill constantly and creatively as the marriage continues.

Only in this way can there be any realistic hope that married couples may in future succeed in countering all the pressures forcing them apart. Only in this way can they grow together and find fulfilment in a lifelong marriage. Only in this way can families regain the stability that comes from stable marriages. *Courage* to confront pinches seems to me an essential Christian family value.

Taking stock

If you would like to pray about *courage* in confronting pinches and resolving conflict you could go on with the parable of the merciful father.

Becoming quiet
Become quiet in your thoughts and relaxed in your body.

The grace

Father, help married people to deal with the pinches in their relationships. Help them not to ignore pinches, but with courage to bring them to their partner and seek a solution.

The story

While he was still a long way off, his father saw him and was moved with pity. He ran to the boy, clasped him in his arms and kissed him tenderly. Then his son said, 'Father, I have sinned against heaven and against you. I no longer deserve to be called your son.' But the father said to his servants, 'Quick! Bring out the best robe and put it on him; put a ring on his finger and sandals on his feet. Bring the calf we have been fattening, and kill it; we are going to have a feast, a celebration, because this son of mine was dead and has come back to life; he was lost and is found.' And they began to celebrate.

Now the elder son was out in the fields, and on his way back, as he drew near the house, he could hear music and dancing. Calling one of the servants he asked what it was all about. 'Your brother has come' replied the servant 'and your father has killed the calf we had fattened because he has got him back safe and sound.' He was angry then and refused to go in, and his father came out to plead with him; but he answered his father, 'Look, all these years I have slaved for you and never once disobeyed your orders, yet you never offered me so much as a kid for me to celebrate with my friends. But, for this son of yours, when he comes back after swallowing up your property—he and his women—you kill the calf we had been fattening.'

The father said, 'My son, you are with me always and all I have is yours. But it was only right we should celebrate and rejoice, because your brother here was dead and has come to life; he was lost and is found.'

Luke 15

Bringing it home

There are two stories here. First see the dusty road, feel the sun beating down. Put yourself into the picture as the younger son, walking home rehearsing your party piece. Feel the ache in your legs, the sand in your eyes, nose and mouth. Try to guess how your father will receive you. Are you fearful? Ashamed? Hopeful? Or how do you feel? Allow yourself to be over-whelmed with relief as your father goes right over the top in his joy and delight and celebration. Feel your self-respect return-ing as you are reinstated in your rightful place.

Next see the fields where the elder son is working. See the shadows lengthen, feel the air getting colder. Become the elder son as you finish work. Maybe feel the sweat cooling on your brow, and the ache in your back as you straighten your shoulders. Sounds of music reach your ears: what can you hear? Listen to the servant's explanation and feel your resentment and anger. Tune into how you feel about having your own point of view so totally ignored.

Now go over the story again. Notice how you feel as each brother in turn. Have a conversation with Jesus the storyteller about your experience.

Some thoughts for today's families

After all the feasting the two sons would have had to live together and co-operate in running the farm. Remembering that real peace is based on justice and truth whereas 'peace and quiet' is a false peace, can you imagine any way they could work together harmoniously? They would be under their father's loving and watchful eye—what difference would that make? Has this anything to teach Christians concerned about marriage today?

If you have made marriage vows and have managed to keep them you have something in common with the elder son who never once disobeyed his father's orders. Turn to God your Father and tell him how you feel about those who don't keep their vows today. If you've not been able to keep your marriage vows try telling the Father what you feel about those who have. If you have never married tell the Father what you feel about both groups.

Read again the ten points which make for successful reso-lution of pinches. Can you take up some pinch with the person who is causing it?

Chapter 6
PICK UP YOUR STRETCHER

Spontaneity is vital in human relationships. When we are happy and life is going well, good relating seems to come bubbling out of us. Our instincts, our emotions and our reason seem in harmony. Our dealings with those we love seem to be ours and ours alone. Our touch is secure, our behaviour confident. Others catch our mood and respond happily, and we feel our lives enriched. We should certainly resent any suggestion that our way of relating could be reduced to a pat formula.

Sometimes, doing and saying what comes naturally does not seem to work. Relating to those we love seems more difficult. If the difficulty becomes long-standing we may not see how to get out of it. Trying to puzzle out what is wrong may yield only pain and confusion.

Then it can help to strip away the flesh of relating and look at the bones. We can see how they fit together, what makes them work. Often we can see where trouble lies and how it can be remedied. Then each of us can reclothe the bones of our relating with our own individual flesh, and continue to relate to those we love in our own unique way.

I have found the clearest way to see how a marriage works is Sherwood and Glidewell's PINCH/CRUNCH flowchart. I have introduced this at many meetings and reproduced it in other

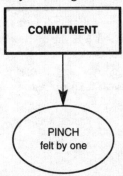

Figure 1 Pinches arise in every committed relationship

books. To some people it is a revelation: they look at all the ways of dealing with a pinch, take in the options and outcomes at a glance. A light dawns and they say 'Now I see!' Others, perhaps the majority, like to have the flowchart built up for them bit by bit. No single connection is at all complicated or difficult to understand. Piece by piece the flowchart builds up into a clear overview of how a marriage works, and what happens when it doesn't. Even if you are not usually at home with diagrams, it is worth staying with this one as I fit it together here one piece at a time. It starts with a married couple. One of them feels a pinch.

Marriages thrive and grow stronger through open and honest negotiation of pinches. Pinches are inevitable in every marriage, and this is indicated by the solid arrow in Figure 1.

Today people expect more from marriage yet have to adapt to many more changes. No wonder they feel more pinches and today's marriages have become more fragile. Yet wives or

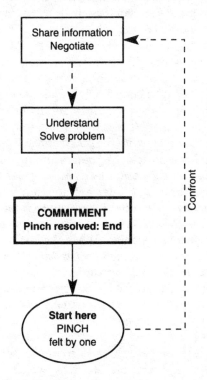

Figure 2 Successful resolution of a pinch

husbands are not helpless. They can counter this fragility by learning to confront their partner.

The person feeling the pinch can raise the issue and explain the trouble, both can discuss it and think of different ways to cope with it, they can understand each other's viewpoint and find a joint solution. Then they can return to a deeper commitment than before. As long as they are willing to make time for it, such confrontation is possible for most couples most of the time. As shown in Figure 2, it is an active way of keeping a marriage alive.

Stability reached after resolving a pinch cannot last. Very soon another pinch is felt by one of the partners, and the whole process starts again. Pinches are perfectly normal and occur in all relationships. There is no need to panic, to think this should not be happening in a good Christian marriage. The aim is for each pinch in turn to be confronted and resolved without undue delay. This helps a couple to change and grow and ensures that they do it together. Perseverance in confronting pinches is needed today as never before.

The previous chapter has shown how the person feeling the pinch, instead of presenting the difficulty as their own and asking for help, may spoil the confrontation by attacking their partner. This causes the partner to be defensive, and makes it impossible for him or her to understand the pinch and make it a joint problem for the partners to solve together. They dodge the problem and return to commitment with the pinch unresolved.

There is another obstacle to understanding and problem-solving. This is when experience leads one partner to be already heavily defensive, and they interpret any confrontation as an attack. All of us have favourite defences which we hide behind when under stress. We use *denial* when we refuse to accept that unpleasant things are happening. When we just blank them out we use *repression*. Some of us show *regression* by becoming childish and helpless in the face of difficulty, expecting others to cope. Sometimes we set up the smokescreen of *displacement* and chatter on about irrelevant matters or take out on our partner anger caused by somebody else.

Sometimes we *generalize* by making sweeping statements about others or *project* the blame on to someone else or *rationalize* by giving endless specious reasons why we are not at fault. Maybe we cover our sadness by acting the clown in *reaction formation.* Maybe we use the defence of *identification* by refusing to speak simply from our own heart but replying instead in other people's words or in platitudes.

These defence measures are largely unconscious, but wives and husbands can soon recognize their partner's favourite defence because he or she keeps repeating it. The way to cope with it is first to avoid name-calling like Liar! Baby! Feather-brain! Clown! or Pompous Ass!, even though these seem richly deserved. The aim then is to give reassurance which meets the fear triggering the defence, so that the defence is not necessary.

For instance, regression might be met with 'I know you find this difficult. I'll help you face it. I'm sure we can work it out together. Just now I'm asking you to look at this problem of mine.'

It seems unfair that the person declaring the pinch must work so hard to get a hearing, but if they will make the effort even

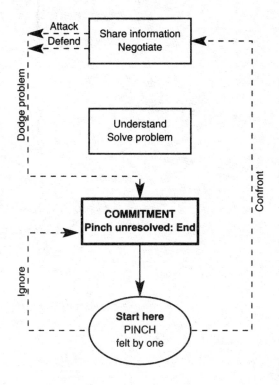

Figure 3 Ignoring pinches, attacking your partner or defending your-self all leave pinches to fester unresolved

a very defensive person can be successfully confronted. Understanding and problem-solving can follow, and the couple need not dodge the problem and return to commitment with the pinch unresolved in the manner illustrated in Figure 3.

Saving up pinches inevitably stores resentment and anger which finally comes out in the relationship. Now the marriage becomes critical, and neither partner knows what to expect of the other. A volatile situation arises as the marriage heads for a crunch.

A crunch exists when the marriage is overtly unhappy. Both partners feel it, and the behaviour of each tends to make the other's behaviour more extreme. For instance, she attacks him so that he withdraws into himself, and the more he withdraws the more she tries to provoke a response by attacking. Or he

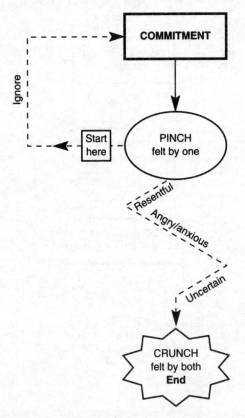

Figure 4 Unresolved pinches can end in a crunch

drinks because she is unfaithful and she is unfaithful because he drinks. There are many possible combinations of unhappiness, where each partner's maddening behaviour tends to feed on the other's as in Figure 4.

Often crunches are punctuated by good resolutions. The couple recall their past love, their children's needs, their Christian faith, and they decide to turn over a new leaf. They declare a truce, kiss and make up, and return to their original commitment. Unfortunately, nothing is changed. The original pinch recurs, the marriage becomes critical once more, and with a sense of helplessness and inevitability the couple slide again into a well-rehearsed crunch, as in Figure 5.

Crunches are too painful a state to remain in for ever. Some-

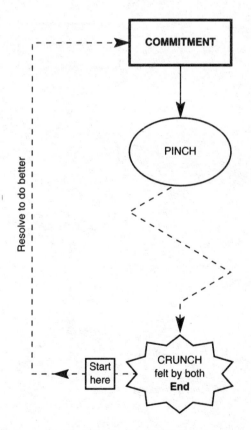

Figure 5 Good resolutions are not enough to get out of a crunch

times the partners withdraw and lead their own lives, although they still remain married. They may decide to stay together for the sake of the children or respectability or money or their religion, but the marriage is emotionally dead.

Many couples, after recurring crunches, recognize that their marriage has ended and finish it legally by divorce. These divorces are characterized by rancour and aggression. 'She took me to the cleaners' and 'He left me with nothing but worry' are typical. Wife and husband part, and both feel wronged and bitter, as in Figure 6.

There is another, more hopeful way out of a crunch. This is when a couple are able to stand aside from their mutual blame and destruction and can actually confront their unresolved pinches. It is extremely difficult to do this without help.

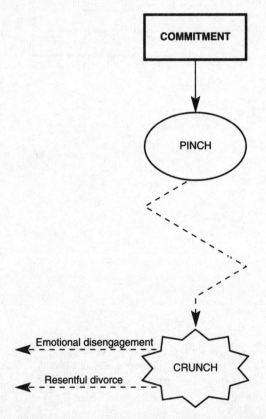

Figure 6 Unresolved crunches lead to divorce or estrangement

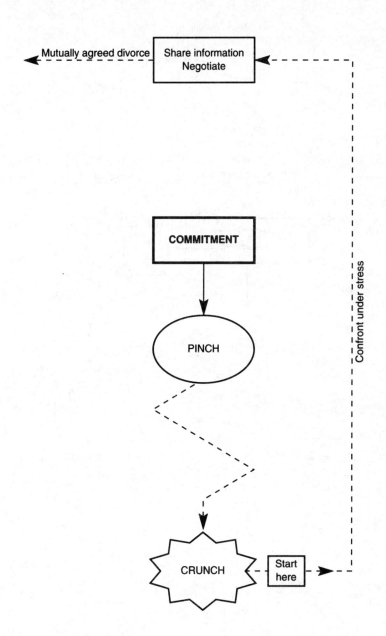

Figure 7 Marriage counsellors or conciliators can help couples to divorce less destructively

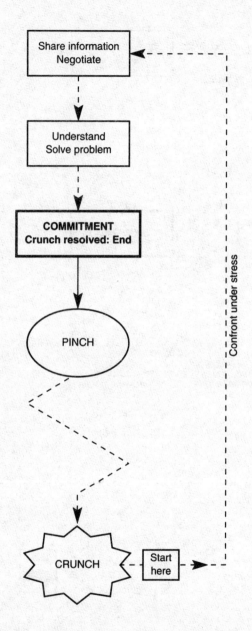

Figure 8 Confronting a crunch is difficult but it can sometimes be successful and the marriage can be saved

Such couples need a skilled person who holds the ring and prevents them from destroying each other. Then they feel safe enough to bring painful issues to light and try to look at them squarely. This is the kind of service offered by RELATE, CMAC and other marriage counsellors. Marriage counsellors help couples to confront long-unresolved pinches to see if their relationship can be salvaged and the marriage saved.

There is no guarantee of success. Yet if parting is inevitable a counsellor can often help couples to manage it more constructively. A runaway emotional situation may be checked. The couple may gain some insight into the reasons for the breakdown, and with understanding comes a measure of forgiveness. The way is paved for conciliation, in which sensible decisions can be made about dividing the money and the continuing support and upbringing of children, as in Figure 7.

The hope is that confronting their problems will enable a couple to understand and solve them. Marriage counsellors see many couples who have been to crunch point and yet are able, with help, to face and resolve their problems and restart their marriage on a new basis, as in Figure 8.

Figure 9 summarizes all the options and shows how a marriage works. Notice that the line between COMMITMENT and PINCH is the only solid line in the whole diagram. This is because pinches are inevitable in every marriage. Crunches are not. Only when pinches are repeatedly ignored or dodged does a marriage become endangered and reach a crunch. This need not happen if couples persevere with sorting out their pinches.

Being with couples in trouble, helping them to understand and forgive each other and plan for the future, sometimes seeing them save their marriage and start afresh—these are the rewards of marriage counsellors. Yet a lifetime with CMAC leads me to ask how we can stop marriages getting into trouble.

Who is helping the couples in good enough marriages? Who is convincing them that forgiving their partner is fine but that they are called to go beyond forgiveness? Who is showing them how to sort out the pinches before they become crunches? Who is encouraging them to sort out a pinch as soon as it arises, so that constantly they feel the warmth and reward of genuinely deepened commitment? Who is helping them to persevere in confronting pinches, so that their marriage grows stronger than all the forces conspiring to pull it apart?

Some of the agencies offering such help will be highlighted

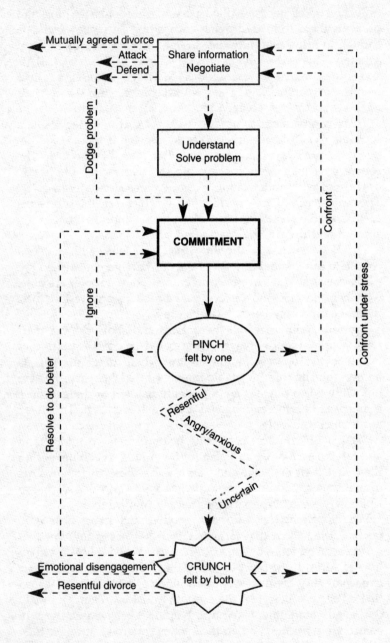

Figure 9 How a marriage works and when it doesn't
(adapted from Sherwood and Glidewell)

in the final chapter. The next chapter calls for this help to be made more accessible to ordinary couples. Marriage breakdown is bad for couples, bad for children, bad for families and bad for society. Never have we been in greater need of the Christian family value of *perseverance* in confronting every pinch as it occurs.

Taking stock

The story of Jesus curing a paralysed man at Capernaum is helpful if you want to pray about *perseverance* in going beyond forgiveness and confronting pinches.

Becoming quiet

Allow your mind to become still and your body to relax.

The grace

Father, we pray for perseverance. Make us ever ready to forgive each other and to work daily to put things right.

The story

Some people came bringing him a paralytic carried by four men, but as the crowd made it impossible to get the man to him they stripped the roof over the place where Jesus was; and when they had made an opening, they lowered the stretcher on which the paralytic lay. Seeing their faith, Jesus said to the paralytic, 'My child, your sins are forgiven'.

Now some scribes were sitting there, and they thought to themselves, 'How can this man talk like that? He is blaspheming. Who can forgive sins but God?' Jesus, inwardly aware that this was what they were thinking, said to them, 'Why do you have these thoughts in your hearts? Which of these is easier: to say to the paralytic, "Your sins are forgiven" or to say, "Get up, pick up your stretcher and walk"?

'But to prove to you that the Son of Man has authority on earth to forgive sins'—he said to the paralytic—'I order you: get up, pick up your stretcher, and go off home.' And the man got up, picked up his stretcher at once and walked out

in front of everyone, so that they were all astounded and
praised God saying, 'We have never seen anything like this'.

Mark 2

Bringing it home

A crowded house. Peer in through the doorway. What can you
see? Feel the heat coming from the bodies inside. Sniff the hot,
stale air. Can you see Jesus at all, or hear him in the background?
Hear the bustle and confusion as the four friends try to get in,
carrying the paralysed man.

Now put yourself in the picture. Are you a bystander? Or
one of the four? Or the paralysed man? Perhaps you could place
on the stretcher a loved one whose marriage concerns you at
the moment. Or perhaps you could place there a problem in
your own marriage that seems insoluble.

Notice how you feel about the extraordinary method of
entry—alarmed? embarrassed? desperate perhaps? Hear Jesus'
words of forgiveness and notice their effect. Hear Jesus' command to go beyond forgiveness, and tune into your feelings as
the paralysed man gets up.

Go over the story again in your mind. Notice how you feel.
Watch Jesus. Talk with him about your experience.

Some thoughts for today's families

Jesus' first words were 'My child, your sins are forgiven'. If we
take this to heart we will not need to defend ourselves or to
blame others. Can you think of an instance where defending or
blaming made it impossible to resolve a problem? Can you try
to act when appropriate as a forgiven person, cutting out the
blame and the defence?

Many married couples do not realize that they need not lie
helplessly paralysed by their problems. It is often possible to
take them up and deal with them. Can you think of a pinch
you took up and resolved successfully? Can you determine to
go on practising taking up pinches and resolving them?

Some people with troubled marriages may need to ask a
counsellor they can trust to help them find healing. Who could
they approach? What would be needed to get them there? Is
there any way you could smooth their path?

Chapter 7
STARTING TO FILL
THE WATERPOTS

Jesus at Cana started to help two young people in trouble by asking servants to fill some waterpots. Why were the pots empty? John tells us that they were used to hold water for Jewish ritual washing. A crowd of guests had gathered, the rituals had been observed, the water had been used and the pots were now empty.

Young couples marry in Christian churches today with high hopes. They have the benefit of everything that tradition, custom and religion can offer. In particular, they are told by the churches that marriage is a commitment to mutual love that is to be faithful and lifelong.

With dismay we realize that telling them is not enough. For increasing numbers all that tradition, custom and religion have given them is not enough. 40 per cent of them seem headed inexorably for divorce, and many of the survivors seem to live far from the community of life and love that marriage is supposed to be. What more can we do?

'Fill the waterpots with water.' I sometimes imagine the servants at Cana going into a well-rehearsed routine typical of many of us in the Christian churches. 'What, again? We've done that once. It made no difference that we can see. It's these young people nowadays. Utterly careless of their responsibilities. Never a thought for the way they've been brought up. Heads full of sex and living together and music and money and pleasing themselves. Give up at the first little difficulty. Of course, if they listened to us . . .'

Jesus calls upon us who say we are his servants. No need to dwell on what went before. We catch his sense of urgency. Fill the pots again. While you do it, look again at your resources. What else can you offer? What could you draw out now from your store, so that his work of transformation can begin?

In our Christian communities we have great resources. Many of them are already used with varying levels of enthusiasm to serve married couples and families. Highlighting good practice may point to treasures we could draw out now.

I hesitate to recommend social and political action, for Christians seem rather ready to mobilize in individual moral crusades and rather reluctant to join with others of goodwill to ensure that marriages and families have the support they need. Yet Christians with a social conscience are the backbone of many voluntary organizations that help families. They are also beginning to be heard and respected when they speak up for families in the political arena.

Some politicians see today's family as failing in its functions, as having off-loaded its responsibilities. I do not myself believe that this is generally so. It is certainly true that in times past the family acted as school, hospital and welfare agency for its members, whereas now we expect these functions to be performed by the state, locally or nationally. Yet these very state services were created because families and their representatives needed and wanted them. At their best, state services are families carrying out their responsibilities by collective means. Most families exercise considerable ingenuity in getting what their members need and are entitled to, from the services available.

Cutbacks in public services increase the strain on all families to some extent, but at any one time we are not equal consumers of public services. A healthy, childless couple who are both at work may hardly notice the cuts; a family where the father has been made redundant, the daughter cannot find work and the mother cares for a son with Down's syndrome will find every cut another blow, another unexpected burden.

Current policy with regard to employment and taxation can also bear heavily on families. Unemployed men have higher death rates, crime rates and divorce rates than those that are in work. Increased VAT is a disproportionate burden for poorer families, because taxed necessities must be bought regardless of ability to pay.

Political and social policy are controversial matters and even among Christians it is not possible to find easy unanimity. Yet if we profess concern for the family we are bound to ask what is our responsibility as voters, as political and social activists, as citizens in a democratic society when we see such stresses falling today on the families least able to bear them. If any collective service is failing families what should be our collective response?

If we want the family to carry its responsibilities, its members must not be broken in their efforts to find the means. The family and the wider society have mutual responsibilities, and when our society fails our families the voice of the Christian churches is starting to be heard. When there are calls to keep religion out of politics the Christian churches remember those political words of Jesus about the hungry, thirsty, naked, homeless, outcast, sick and imprisoned people of his day: 'insofar as you did this to one of the least of these brothers of mine, you did it to me'.

Within Christian communities there are many groups which support families: pre-school children are eased into the wider society while their mothers get a break, mothers and toddlers share tea and games and a chat, single parents gain the strength of mutual support and help. There are clubs for young people and day centres for the elderly. There are family groups and baby-sitting circles. There are groups for keeping fit, for handicrafts, for DIY, and for cookery.

Thrift clubs and credit unions, second-hand clothes exchanges and jumble sales, social clubs and dances, parish barbecues and fish and chip suppers, picnics and coach trips—all this and much more is still organized by the Christian churches. If all the church halls in the country were to shut down tomorrow the daily life of many families would be immeasurably impoverished. If all the church halls in the country were to copy the good practice of the best, the daily life of many families would be immensely enriched.

Family liturgies are on the increase. I am most familiar with those in Roman Catholic churches but I know that all the churches are making new efforts to celebrate and cater for different aspects of family life. In some places, while older people listen to Scripture readings and a homily, the small children have their own liturgy of the Word before joining their parents for the Eucharist. At other services young people lead the singing and music and act or mime gospel stories for the congregation. Opportunities are taken to celebrate silver and golden weddings, and marriage vows are renewed.

Special celebrations of married love, such as those pioneered by Jack Dominian, are becoming better known. It is good to hear clear words in praise of married sexual love in the setting of a church service; it will be even better when liturgists and local people follow this example and get together to praise God for marriage in their own way and their own words.

Political, social and liturgical action can all help support marriage and the family. Yet if my thesis is correct the greatest threat to the family today is that so many couples find it difficult to persevere in their married relationship. If the Christian churches really want to be effective here, what else can we draw from our treasure? How else may we serve marriage?

The Christian churches have learned much from the human and behavioural sciences. Already in our church practice we have experience of three important ways of strengthening relationships. The first is to enable young people to grow in self-awareness, self-esteem and the ability to relate well. The second is to help couples just before a wedding to clarify their shared values, agree their roles and manage conflict. The third is to be with married people at times of stress and change, helping them to adjust and go forward with confidence.

Education in personal relationships is no longer experimental. It has a firm place in most schools which even the National Curriculum is finding hard to usurp. Pupils benefit from it and teachers see the need for it. Youth leaders and retreat givers find it one of their most popular activities. At its best it can help young people to understand themselves and to become confident, independent adults who can make informed choices and relate skilfully and responsibly.

For nearly half a century CMAC has been at the forefront of relationships education for young people. Its collective experience is drawn on in Margaret Vincent's book *Love Needs Learning*. If we want more couples to come to marriage with the ability to relate well, the Christian churches will need to look for every means to extend and enhance education in relationships for all our young people.

Marriage preparation has long been my interest and throughout the 1980s it was my job to help train parish marriage preparation teams on behalf of CMAC. We had a vision of local married people who would welcome and show an interest in every couple asking to marry in their parish church. They would give them a chance to talk about topics which couples marrying often skirt around, like money, work, sex, religion and the place of children in a marriage.

This was not an optimum scheme to be run by experts for a few highly-motivated couples. Like the barefoot doctors of the

Third World our parish couples would learn just a few skills and cope with just a few topics. They would offer a simple and effective marriage preparation which became part of the normal package for everyone getting married in their church.

Barefoot marriage preparation. Who are the best people to offer it? Our shopping list looked like this:

Profile of people suitable for parish marriage teams

friendly and outgoing

married about ten years

comfortable in their marriage

willing to give the equivalent of one weekend for training

ready to spend ten evenings a year with couples marrying locally

concerned to help others form a married relationship that will endure and grow in love

ready to co-operate with the parish clergy

When I showed this profile to parish clergy the first reaction was that they didn't have anybody like this. Especially, they didn't have any couples so young. When I asked who were the mothers who met their children at the infant school gates, or the fathers who were bringing their babies for baptism, suddenly a whole new group became visible. Not the usual pillars of the church who organize everything, but a younger group who are pleased to be invited to serve in this way and who have the great advantage of not talking down to the couples getting married.

When volunteers came for training I would ask them what they thought couples getting married need most. The list was long and impressive. But barefoot volunteers have to be ruthless. Out went all the items smacking of good advice or wise precept: advice is often given but rarely taken. Out went all the 'expert' topics like banking, conveyancing, family planning or medical advice: if individual couples need these there are qualified experts they can consult. Out went anything looking too far ahead, like coping with your teenager, mid-life crisis or retirement: couples won't remember it for years and put it into practice later. Their best guarantee of making good choices later is to practise negotiating tricky areas in their relationship now. So what's left? Three themes are vital.

The first examines the whole area of a couple's values. What is important to this couple? What is their marriage going to

stand for? Parish volunteers help them look at their own prefer-
ences and each other's, from how many sugars in her tea and
whether or not he likes football, to the importance of religious
practice to each partner.

The second topic looks at the roles of wife and husband. Who
will make the morning tea, get the shopping, clean the lavatory
or put out the rubbish? How will they handle money? How
will they relate sexually? What place will children have in their
marriage? At a time when the roles of husbands and wives are
so ambiguous it is vital that couples sort out before their wedding the division of labour that suits them. It is also vital that
they have experience of the way to negotiate and change such
an understanding.

Finally volunteers help couples getting married to cope with
conflict, to sort out pinches before they become crunches, to go
beyond forgiveness to the true reconciliation that comes with
solving joint problems fairly. A parish volunteer who tells
couples how to be married is soon forgotten. One who helps
couples to practise confronting each other without fear or
aggression gives them a skill which may last them till death.

I am convinced that if every couple marrying in a Christian
church faced up to clarifying their values and roles and learnt
how to manage conflict then far more marriages would get off
to a good start. Yet starting is one thing, coping with change
and persevering through hard times is another. It seems to me
that an admirable opportunity for serving husbands and wives
at times of change and stress occurs when they ask for their
children to receive the sacraments of Baptism, Eucharist and
Confirmation.

In most Roman Catholic churches preparing for sacraments is
now a community affair, and parents are as involved as their
children. Nor is the preparation trivial: in many schemes parents
meet regularly for the best part of a year. Together they discover
where God is at work in their own world, in their families and
in their daily lives. Together they share their experiences of
bringing up children, coping with hardship and trying to keep
their married relationship fresh.

Many parents find that the preparation of their children for
sacraments marks a turning point in their own lives. For some
it reveals a new face of the church: for the first time they
experience a church interested in their lives, keen to hear their
opinions and their unique experience, valuing their contribution,

understanding their daily struggles and joys. Most parents say they come to the meetings for their children's sake but stay for their own. I think it may be possible to extend these schemes.

Baptism which occurs soon after the birth of a baby offers an opportunity to explore how the family is adjusting. How is the baby settling down? Are the parents remembering each other's needs in the face of their baby's demands? Can they still have time out together? A study of European Values showed that the group with the least sense of well-being were mothers at home with small children. Baptism preparation is a good time to check what measures a family are able to take for the mother to keep in touch with the wider world.

When children are preparing for the Eucharist their parents can benefit from reviewing their roles. Do they share the child care, and agree on how it should be carried out? Do they still have time for each other? Where and how do they sort out their differences? Do they still manage to have fun together? Is their marriage going in the direction they would like and what plans can they make for the future?

Confirmation often finds parents in some disarray. Children who were biddable now seem more self-willed. Fathers may be running out of steam and feel threatened by a younger generation at work. Mothers sometimes find new interests and challenges which are at odds with their domestic role. Both partners may feel that time is running out for them to fulfil the dreams they once had. It can be a great help to talk with other wives and husbands in the same situation, and to hear their plans and strategies for coping.

It should not be too difficult to develop sacramental preparation with a view to strengthening the parents' marriage at these critical stages. It seems an ideal opportunity to help those parents to adapt to change and to show them new opportunities for growth in their marriage. This would have to be done in a way that did not discriminate against those families without two married parents. It might also mean that where catechists are unmarried they would have to co-opt married couples as leaders, to help prepare material relevant to married life and love.

I have little experience of preparing people for these sacraments; so I must leave to others the details of how sacramental schemes can be extended. Catechists are very creative and inventive people. They serve children well by preparing them for sacraments. I venture to suggest that children would be served even better if at the same time their parents' marriage could be made more secure and loving.

Service is the Christian family value highlighted in this chapter. The Christian churches have many opportunities to serve families. We can help people to persevere in marriage, but only if our political, social and liturgical action is supplemented by something more. We must help people to grow in their ability to relate as young people, as couples about to marry and as married people developing and changing throughout the years.

Taking stock

Prayer on the theme of *service* to the married relationship can be built around the story of Jesus washing his disciples' feet.

Becoming quiet

Allow your mind to become quiet and your body to relax.

The grace

Father, let us be ready to serve you in the married people we meet. Show us how to help them to live in love.

The story

> Jesus . . . got up from table, removed his outer garment and, taking a towel, wrapped it round his waist; he then poured water into a basin and began to wash the disciples' feet and to wipe them with the towel he was wearing.
>
> He came to Simon Peter, who said to him, 'Lord, are you going to wash my feet?' Jesus answered, 'At the moment you do not know what I am doing, but later you will understand'. 'Never!' said Peter. 'You shall never wash my feet.' Jesus replied, 'If I do not wash you, you can have nothing in common with me'. 'Then, Lord,' said Simon Peter 'not only my feet, but my hands and my head as well!' Jesus said, 'No one who has taken a bath needs washing, he is clean all over. You too are clean, though not all of you are.' He knew who was going to betray him, that was why he said, 'though not all of you are'.
>
> When he had washed their feet and put on his clothes

again he went back to the table. 'Do you understand' he
said 'what I have done to you? You call me Master and Lord,
and rightly; so I am. If I, then, the Lord and Master, have
washed your feet, you should wash each other's feet. I
have given you an example so that you may copy what
I have done to you.'

John 13

Bringing it home

You are in an upper room. How is it furnished? The twelve
companions are preparing for a festive meal. What can you see?
Smell? Taste? Hear? There is a sense of danger—how does it
show?

Now put yourself into the scene. Are you Peter? Or perhaps
another of the twelve? Or the often weary person you are today?
Notice how you react when Jesus puts the towel round his waist
and turns to you? Feel him massaging away the efforts and cares
of the day. Feel his concern for your callouses, your blisters, all
the sore, abraded and sensitive areas. Allow him to do a really
thorough job. Feel the comfort of your tended feet as you slip
them back into your sandals. Does having your feet washed by
Jesus change the way you feel about yourself? What do you
want to say to Jesus afterwards?

Go over the story again in your mind. Notice how you feel.
Watch Jesus. Talk to him about your experience.

Some thoughts for families today

Be with Jesus as he puts a towel round your waist and asks
you to kneel with a bowl of water to wash the feet of people
in families you know. What corns, blisters and sores have they
collected on their journey? Ask Jesus to show you the best way
to help them feel understood and restored.

What services to help families does your local church offer?
Do they meet people's needs? Are more volunteers needed?

Could your local church offer any other service which would
help married people to cope better at critical times for their
family? What could you do to help bring this about?

Chapter 8

FILLING TO THE BRIM

During the 1980s I travelled all over the country training young married couples who volunteered to work as parish marriage preparation teams. They were responsive to the idea of helping intending wives and husbands to clarify their values and goals and to manage conflict. Perhaps the hardest thing I asked of them was to help couples getting married to look at why they chose to marry in this particular church.

Why was this so difficult? The reason was simple. Volunteers are usually highly committed to their church, so much so that they are willing to take on this extra ministry. The couples getting married mostly are not.

A few couples who marry in Roman Catholic churches are used to church ways—either they are both practising Catholics or they are genuine two-church couples. But most couples asking to marry in our churches are not at all like that. Instead, one partner tends to have some loose family connection with the Catholic church but little personal commitment to it or familiarity with its language and practice. The other partner has no particular religion at all but agrees to go through with a church wedding for the sake of being obliging.

Why are they asking to marry in church? Reasons vary from 'I wouldn't feel married if I didn't' through 'It seems to make the occasion more special, somehow' to 'My family expect it' and 'It makes a better setting for the videos'. Why does the church agree to marry them? Because they present the church with a genuine pastoral opportunity, and because their commitment to each other is for us a sign of God's presence that the church community can joyfully recognize and celebrate. Yet the church agreeing to marry them does present a challenge to the volunteers trying to prepare them.

Can parish volunteers accept each couple coming for marriage as they are, and not try to fit them into a churchy mould? Can they trust that God is present in the love of couples coming for marriage, without insisting on churchy ways of expressing this?

Can they recognize this presence of God and celebrate it joyfully, without insisting on sticking Christian labels all over it? Can they help deepen the undoubted commitment which couples have for each other, rather than demand a commitment to Christianity which many couples do not pretend to have? Can parish volunteers do all this and still be true to their own Christian vision of marriage?

I helped parish couples to meet this challenge with three exercises built from each couple's own experience. The exercises could be done equally by believers or unbelievers, in fact some righteous people were scornful and asked 'Where's the religion in that? What has that to do with God?' Yet the exercises succeeded in giving the volunteers a new and joyful view of their own marriages and they felt confident to use them later with couples getting married.

In today's world people are hungry for a new vision of marriage. The present search for Christian family values is also looking for a new vision, as we look for other resources to draw from our Christian store. We respond to Christ's call, we start to fill the waterpots anew. We set out to help young people to learn to relate, couples marrying to clarify their values and roles and to manage conflict, and married people to change and grow together. And then we fill the pots to the brim. We look for signs of God's presence in the experience of married life. We pour out the plain and honest water of being married and, between one blink and the next, see the pots brimful of God's joy and life and power.

What are the three exercises that help bring this about? How do the parish volunteers reach this new vision? Their first exercise is to recollect what Maslow calls 'peak experiences'. This is enjoyable for most married couples, who love to recall their shared history. They look over their lives since they first met. Each couple spends time together picking out the special moments. Important. Significant. Times that matter. I try to avoid the clichés. I know that popular songs have long been engaged in the same search, for magic moments and occasions when time stood still.

It is a constant delight how readily married couples invest the clichés with real meaning, or steer round the banal and bring their own experiences freshly minted to share with their colleagues. 'We picnicked on a cliff top overlooking the sea. The sun set over the water. We felt utterly at peace.' 'We were decorating our first house. We sat on packing cases and ate fish and chips out of newspaper. It was the best meal I'd ever tasted.' 'I drove through the night with my wife and children asleep in the car. I realized that all I love was there, entrusted to me.' 'We sat either side of our son's hospital bed. We knew he was very ill. We felt totally united in our will to help him. We seemed to hold our breath together, and hope.'

Christians have a name for what is ultimately special, significant, outside time. Christians call that God. None of the examples quoted are churchy. None of the married people refer to God directly. Yet can a believer doubt that God is present or say that God is not at work here? Recollecting their peak experiences can remind married people that marriage can give a taste of God through the deep experiences shared by a husband and wife.

This exercise is powerful for couples where one is a Christian and one is not. Both can agree about the significance of their peak experiences. He may call it God's presence while she calls it an important time which they shared, but somehow religion ceases to be a no-go area between them. They recognize that Christians simply use different words to talk about something which is important to them both. Sometimes the Christian words can even help them see and enjoy their experience more clearly.

The next exercise is firmly set in the everyday world. Married couples are asked in what ways they rely on their partner to get them through the day. If their partner went away for a week, or was in hospital for ten days, what practical help would they most miss?

Couples spend some time telling each other this. It can be a revelation. Husbands and wives who feel taken for granted, whose contribution seems only acknowledged by criticism when something goes wrong, at last have the joy of hearing from their partner that they are appreciated, valued and relied upon. Once couples start they can produce many examples of the ways that their partner helps them. As they report these I amuse myself trying to allocate their examples to three separate lists.

The first might look like this: making tea, buying stores, cleaning the lavatory, mending the roof, earning money, putting out the rubbish, doing the accounts, relieving sexual tension, looking after me when I'm ill. On the second list I enter things like calming me down, listening to my day, hearing my worries, making time for me, confirming my masculinity, accepting me as I am, making me laugh, reminding me of other people's feelings. The third list is usually shorter, because of the short-term nature of the original question. It can contain items like planning holidays, decorating the house, encouraging me to dress well, backing my job application, making me feel great in bed, and showing me how to garden.

I make these three lists to show that volunteers have experienced in their own marriages examples of sustaining each other, healing each other and helping each other grow. Dr Jack Dominian has for many years maintained that these are the reasons why couples move from being 'in love' to the less intense but more lasting state of 'loving' that is a lifelong marriage. If they achieve these sufficiently their marriage will last and be successful. If not, the marriage is set to fail.

Sustaining in marriage comprises all the things that good parents do for their children, but makes them appropriate to adulthood, so that a wife and husband look after each other and provide for each other, making each other feel loved and wanted. *Healing* offers a second chance to right the things that went wrong in that first relationship with parents, so that in marriage anxious people can grow confident, childish people become responsible and neglected people feel cherished. *Growth* in marriage is evident when couples help each other to accept new challenges, take on new responsibilities, confront and solve problems and grow together in spite of all the changes forcing them apart. The three lists help married people see that all this activity is already taking place in their own marriages.

We can go further. Christians believe that sustaining is the work of God the Father, creator and sustainer of all. Healing is the work of God the Son, and growth the work of God's life-giving Spirit. We Christians can then see God at work in all these marriages; in matters as mundane as putting out the rubbish, listening to the day's events or backing a job application we can recognize our threefold God. Marriage becomes a way of experiencing God as Father, Son and Spirit whenever husband and wife sustain each other, heal each other and help each other grow.

A final exercise in search of a new vision of marriage comes from considering the implications of the PINCH/CRUNCH model of the way marriages work. This view of marriage asks a lot from married people. It asks them to have courage, to recognize when something in their relationship is amiss, to speak up and say 'it's not working, is it?' It asks them to have humility, to realize that they are not perfect and that they may disappoint or hurt their partner, to listen and to accept that there may be truth in their partner's confrontation. It asks them to be creative in solving each difficulty, in working out a new way to get on together.

It asks them to persevere, to be ever ready to take up any difference that arises between them, to talk about it and to resolve it. When we explain the PINCH/CRUNCH model to people asking to marry in our churches we Christians are calling them to daily conversion, repentance and change. We call them to be permanently committed to a love which is ever seeking true reconciliation.

This is the heart of our belief about marriage. John says in his first letter:

> No one has ever seen God;
> but as long as we love one another
> God will live in us
> and his love will be complete in us.

At the heart of our belief are three Persons in a relationship of love; that love is at work in the peak experiences of marriage, in the ordinary mutual caring of wives and husbands, and in their efforts to be daily reconciled.

This is a lofty meaning for marriage. The Christian churches are right to set this ideal before us, that marriage can be, is meant to be, a community of life and love which shares in the joy and life and love of God. Yet it is an ideal with a high price.

This ideal for marriage has hitherto been bought at the price of increased marital breakdown. The stakes have been permanently raised. More husbands, more wives are now aware that their marriage does not measure up to what it is meant to be. They can see no realistic way to improve, and in their despair they separate and divorce.

Perhaps some of these marriages were from the start fated to fail. Some people are not capable of making and sustaining a close and loving relationship. Some are so ill-matched that loving co-operation is unlikely. Yet many wives and husbands mean well, try hard, suffer much for their marriage. If only they knew how to sort out the pinches before they become crunches, many more could succeed.

If the churches are serious about their ideal of marriage as a community of life and love, a share in the joy and life and love of God, we Christians will care for the casualties and support and strengthen the strugglers. Then we will have earned the right to continue calling most of our people to this ideal. For most people their marriage can be the centre of their spirit's life, their personal way to happiness and bliss. Husbands and wives can still know the strong love described in the Song of Songs:

My Beloved is mine and I am his.

Set me like a seal on your heart,
like a seal on your arm.
For love is strong as Death,
jealousy relentless as Sheol.
The flash of it is a flash of fire,
a flame of Yahweh himself.
Love no flood can quench,
no torrents drown.

The Christian ideal of marriage is needed today more than ever, and we yearn to know that such happiness is still capable of being realized. The Christian family value to call on here is *joy*. As Jesus says:

I have told you this
so that my own joy may be in you
and your joy be complete.
This is my commandment:
love one another
as I have loved you.

John 15

We need to believe with all our hearts that marriage can become a community of life and love, and that this joy can be ours. We need to believe with all our hearts that, just as God's love is for ever, so married love can still last until death.

Taking stock

If you would like to pray for married people everywhere to be touched by this *joy* in their relationship, the transfiguration of Jesus is a mysterious story to ponder.

Becoming quiet

Approach the story with still thoughts and a quiet mind.

The grace

Father, we pray for married people to be touched by your gladness in their relationship with each other. Help us all to know that you have created marriage to give pleasure and joy to your people.

The story

Jesus took with him Peter and James and his brother John and led them up a high mountain where they could be alone. There in their presence he was transfigured: his face shone like the sun and his clothes became as white as the light. Suddenly Moses and Elijah appeared to them; they were talking with him.

Then Peter spoke to Jesus. 'Lord', he said 'it is wonderful for us to be here; if you wish, I will make three tents here, one for you, one for Moses and one for Elijah.'

He was still speaking when suddenly a bright cloud covered them with shadow, and from the cloud there came a voice which said, 'This is my Son, the Beloved; he enjoys my favour. Listen to him.' When they heard this, the disciples fell on their faces, overcome with fear.

But Jesus came up and touched them. 'Stand up', he said 'do not be afraid.' And when they raised their eyes they saw no one but only Jesus.

Matthew 17

Bringing it home

You have just climbed the mountain with Peter, James and John. Drop exhausted in the shade of a rock. Feel its coolness against your sweaty back. Shade your eyes with your hand and squint at Jesus as he stands in the sunlight. As you see Jesus transfigured, let yourself be overwhelmed by the knowledge that

Jesus is special, different. He ranks with Moses and Elijah. Hear Peter babbling about tents, trying to keep the moment for ever. Hear the mysterious voice confirming the certainty which shines out of Jesus: that he is God's beloved. Tell Jesus whatever you can catch of the wonder.

Then perhaps come down from the mountain to the everyday world. Look at the dusty, ordinary Jesus, robes no longer dazzling, face no longer shining. Feel the whisper of sufferings to come. Has your experience on the mountain made any change in the way you look at him now? Talk to Jesus about this.

Allow the story to unfold in your mind. Notice how you feel. Watch Jesus. When the action is over, talk with Jesus about it.

Some thoughts for today's families

'The bride was radiant. The bridegroom beamed widely.' Ordinary people can be transformed when they know they are loved, and their love can warm and delight those around them.

How can we show those around us a vision of the joy and love of marriage? How can we keep hold of the vision in the hard, everyday world? What single change in your life, however small, would help you or those around you to rejoice in the ideal of Christian marriage as a community of life and love?

Chapter 9

THE SERVANTS KNEW

This book is about making families work. It has focused on the married relationship because marriages are the glue which hold families together. When marriages fail, families tend to fall apart. Yet a family extends far beyond a marriage and when marriages break down it is often the wider family which picks up the pieces.

Much of the PINCH/CRUNCH model of marriage applies to any family relationship. Pinches occur in every relationship. If you cannot walk away pinches which are ignored or dodged will lead to a crunch. It is imperative that husbands and wives deal with their pinches; other family members perhaps have greater room for agreeing to differ. Yet parents and children, brothers and sisters, grandparents and grandchildren, all family relationships can benefit when the person feeling a pinch takes it up with courage and confronts the person hurting them, and when both work together to find a solution.

Jesus points to the reward: 'If he listens to you, you have won back your brother.' Families who do not live in the false 'peace and quiet' which papers over cracks but in the true peace which comes from sorting out their problems, can be a sign of hope in a world which longs for peace.

How else can families give hope to the world? I am not sure when I first heard the family described as 'the domestic church': the term is certainly used in a papal statement of 1981 entitled *Familiaris Consortio*. I do know that I greeted the description with derision.

A picture of this domestic church came instantly to my mind. A dinner table spread with a crisp white cloth. Well-behaved children with hands washed and hair neatly brushed sat around, smiling and polite. Heads were bowed and Father said grace. Father carved the joint. Mother served the vegetables: the meal was, of course, perfectly cooked and served, the conversation respectful and edifying.

When this domestic church attended the larger church down

the road it made a considerable impact. Mother, Father and their four well-dressed children took up a whole bench. The other benches were filled with other 'domestic churches', equally clear of eye and clean of clothes.

My own experience was otherwise. Family meals were a struggle. A struggle to cook the food in time. A struggle to sort out squabbles and keep everybody safe and happy while I did so. A struggle to get everyone to come when the food was ready, and not to feed them one at a time 'on the wing' yet again. Grace had long ago been relegated to Christmas and special occasions. Sometimes a meal turned into a special occasion: we all became engrossed in a topic of common interest and the experience of oneness was such that the youngest cried out 'Don't let's finish this meal!', but day-to-day feeding was a rougher affair altogether.

Our appearance at the church down the road was also less than edifying. The usual scramble to get there. The usual disagreement about what the children would wear. And if outward conformity was difficult to achieve, how much more so the interior commitment that we really hoped for as our children's heritage. One by one they slipped away, until one day we found ourselves on the bench as two lone parents and realized that from then on this was how it would be. Our children would have to find their salvation by following whatever they saw to be right; for them this no longer included joining us on that bench and there witnessing to and embodying our family as a domestic church.

Our own experience may explain why I received the expression 'domestic church' with such a jaundiced eye. Yet to view the family as respectable churchgoers who even at home behave in a churchy way scarcely does the expression justice. Changes are happening in the church and in the family. If family and church can be in any way equated, and if Christians want to understand what is happening to the family and continue to place their hope in it, there is much to be gained by drawing on our experience of what is happening to the church.

How can the ordinary Christian think of the church? The physical and social sciences often use models to get a grasp on difficult and abstract concepts. Light, for instance, may be viewed as a wave or as a particle. When viewing it as a wave does not fit the way we experience light to behave, it may be better to drop that view and look upon light as a particle. Both models are analogies: we choose the one that best fits the facts we are considering. Avery Dulles has done something similar with models of the church.

Dulles's first model is the *institution*, the rock-like church of my childhood. Its teachings were clear, its rules were clear, and they were passed from pope to bishops to priests to people. Everyone had their set role within the church, and you knew who was in and who was out.

This institutional church is mirrored by the institution of the family. Traditionally the family had clear rules and clear roles. Authority passed from father to mother to children. Family members knew their duty towards the wider family and whether or not they were living up to the family's expectations.

Institutions give their members certainty and stability but can make them rigid, passive, conformist, defensive, uncreative and rebellious. If we are looking for a better way of being church or being family, let us try another model.

Dulles's next model sees the church as a *community*, either as the body of Christ with the different parts working together in harmony, or as the people of God on their pilgrim way. Equally, the family sets out to be a community working, living and loving together, a body whose members belong as of right and who each make their distinctive contributions to the common good.

Communities can offer their members a sense of belonging, of personal and individual recognition. They can, however, become emotional hothouses in which their members feel stifled. Alternatively, if they fail to provide the promised feeling of belonging they can cause disillusion, frustration and a desire to leave.

A third model sees the church as a *sacrament* or sign of God's presence. God is at work in the world, and the church points to and celebrates the evidence of God's activity. And somehow that very celebration is the occasion of further divine activity.

The sacramental family mirrors the sacramental church. People gain their first understanding of God's creative power from discovering how their own father and mother acted as procreators, their first understanding of God's love from the love of their parents, their first understanding of God's providence from the food on the family table, the clothes on their back, the family roof over their head. And it is through the procreation, love and providing which goes on in families that

God so often appears to choose to pour out his blessings upon humankind.

The sacramental model of church and family encourages loyalty, gratitude and joyful participation. It can however be inward-turning and clannish and may undervalue the presence of God at work in the world outside of church and family.

Dulles's next model sees the church as a *herald* with a message to proclaim. Hear the word, accept it, recognize Christ as Lord and Saviour. The heraldic family would be one which says clearly what it expects, demands a particular response, insists that its members live in a certain way. Heraldic churches and families are good communicators, but they can be demanding, critical and intolerant of weak or deviant members.

A final model sees the church as the world's *servant*. At home in the world, outward-looking, ready to co-operate with all of goodwill, the church in this model brings to the world its belief in the value and ultimate triumph of justice, love and peace. The corresponding family is one which is interested in the wider world, highly political, generous and charitable to others. Servant churches and families foster a sense of responsibility, love and service, yet they can exploit their own members and neglect their well-being.

Using such models helps the Christian avoid a narrow view of church or family: when one model seems oppressive or intolerable another may be nourishing, life-enhancing and full of hope. A priest or minister at odds with the bureaucracy of the institutional church can still thrive as a preacher and find his place in the church viewed as herald. Teenagers who experience the family as cloying and stifling when viewed as a loving community can still appreciate the family seen in its institutional role of offering them food and shelter. A mother trapped in the family as herald and exhausted with telling children how they should behave can be assuaged by the sight of them gathered at a birthday celebration in the manner of the family as sacrament.

Some models of church or family may be more or less appropriate at different times of life. A Christian who spends her active life supporting worthy causes after the model of the servant church may in her final years seek the warmth of the church as loving community. A father who has concentrated on his institutional role as family breadwinner may move with that family to a self-sufficient smallholding: for political and

ecological reasons he feels more comfortable now with the
model of family as servant.

If one particular model finds the nuclear family wanting, often
the extended family fills the gap. The family as institution
often sees grandparents or aunts and uncles providing for
children where their parents cannot. The family as community
sees cots, baby chairs and playpens passing from one branch to
another according to need. The family as sacrament can find
grandparents, in-laws, cousins and unmarried aunts and uncles
all gathered at Christmas round the table of one particular
couple. The family as herald frequently has one special member
who remembers everyone's birthday, right down to cousins and
second cousins. The family as servant can stop each little unit
from becoming self-absorbed: uncles, aunts, cousins who work
for the good of others in the wider world tell of needs waiting
to be met and pass on the love of God experienced within the
family to a world hungry for that love. Where the nuclear family
gives cause for despair, the extended family can offer hope.

No model tells us all about church or family. Both the church
and the family are at the same time institution, community,
sacrament, herald and servant, and much more beside. Christians believe that the spirit of God is moving over the church in
all its models; over the domestic church of the family we can
also look for signs of the spirit.

Can we doubt that the spirit of God is at work in the family
as institution, wherever the family feeds, clothes, shelters and
protects its members? Wherever people make sacrifices from a
sense of family duty, wherever they shape their individual lives
and wishes to accommodate the wants and needs of other family
members, wherever they pour their energy and talents into
helping and supporting the rest of the family, there Christians
can recognize and thank God for the working of the spirit.

We can also see and name the spirit at work wherever families
act as loving communities, where there is a real sense of belonging, where the members care for and sustain each other emotionally, where there are genuine signs of affection. In this model
the family is especially good at fostering individual talents and
bringing out the creative gifts of its members. Often it is aunts
or uncles who first spot the potential of the younger generation.

The family as sacrament specializes in celebration, in Christmas and anniversaries and birthdays, in marking milestones
like starting school or passing exams or moving house or retiring

from work, in finding ways of gathering to weep or laugh together. For those with eyes to see, all these celebrations can point beyond themselves to the God who provides for our lives and destinies and holds us all in the hollow of his hand.

The family as herald specializes in communication, in putting into words its thoughts and aspirations. It keeps in touch with absent members through phone calls, letters and cards. It asks for favourite songs to be played on the radio, complete with dedication 'For my Mum whose birthday is today' or 'For my husband on our first anniversary' or 'For my grandson who starts school this week'. The family as herald keeps in business the commercial card producers for Valentine's and Mother's and Father's Day, for Get Well Soon and Sorry You're Leaving and Enjoy Your New Home and In Deepest Sympathy. It also puts into words more personal tributes: congratulations when a baby is born, a speech at a wedding, sincere sympathy when someone has died. Even the writers of commercial cards know that You Mean More Than Words Can Say: in all these family communications Christians can glimpse the meaning behind the words, the Word of God who is Christ.

The family as servant specializes in charity, justice and peace. Helping others, righting wrongs, working for sick or handicapped or hungry people, saving the whales or the trees or the ozone layer, the family provides a secure base from which members join with others of goodwill. It is to the family in this model that people turn when somebody needs a meal or a bed for the night, when somebody needs respite or special care, when the question arises as to who can foster or adopt a child. Such families are signs of hope to a despairing world. And behind families like these a Christian can catch sight of the God who provides, cares, liberates and saves.

Far from being derisory, the notion of the family as domestic church proves extraordinarily fruitful when taken in conjunction with Avery Dulles's models of the church. Together they seem to show that God is using families extensively as the ordinary means of pouring blessings upon humankind and of revealing God's own nature. This encourages me to suppose that God is with the family, and intends it to survive. It offers hope that the family has a future. Yet my experience of families compels some qualifications.

The family predates the Christian church, exists throughout the world where people are not Christians, and often subsists when people give up any Christian allegiance. There is no question of such families being knowingly church. They certainly do not come together in the name of Christ, and it insults their own truth to imply that they do. What is asserted here is that the spirit of God blows where it wills in all families, and not only in those whose members call themselves Christian.

In all families the earth is being renewed. The privilege of Christians is sometimes to discern, name and celebrate the spirit of God at work, and my analysis of the family as domestic church has tried to do this with regard to families everywhere. In this discerning, naming and celebrating Christians can be like the servants who filled the waterpots at Cana. The bride and groom did not know the source of the excellent wine. Neither did the guests. Nor the steward. But the servants knew.

This is not to claim that the spirit of God works only through families. Many individuals and groups do good in the world, and most family members expend most of their time and energy in settings other than the family. Yet families in all their forms do seem to be potent channels of God's grace and love. It is difficult to imagine viable substitutes.

Consciousness of the family as domestic church does not thereby make Christian families perfect. In Her Majesty's Prisons I meet young men whose Christian family has never given them a stable home, has refused them love and affection, has abused them so badly that they preferred to sleep on the streets. The phrase used to express the absence of all one expects from a family is chilling: 'my family has blanked me' or 'I have blanked my family'. At the same time the chaotic families—families far from the Christian ideal of father and mother married in church, together with their well-brought-up children—sometimes offer a warmth and forgiveness and generosity which would put ideal families to shame.

With these provisos, seeing our own family as a domestic church can help us discover how to focus our lives as Christians. Family prayers may have their place, but our praying goes deeper. All communication within the family is seen as prayer—each please and thank you and sorry and wow! is also a prayer of petition or thanksgiving or contrition or praise. The Scriptures may have their place, but our liturgy of the word goes deeper: every time we tell other family members about our day or the way we are feeling, every time we listen to each other's troubles, every time we remind each other of our shared experiences, the gospel is preached and heard.

Our Eucharist goes deepest of all. Every meal can become for us *the* meal. Each touch and hug, each kiss and embrace, and especially every act of sexual intercourse between husband and wife can say 'This is my body, given for you'. All our work and service for our family can become the way we make good that gift of self.

Far from distorting ordinary family life into churchiness the idea of the family as domestic church shows ordinary family life as already alive with God's presence. In our families the invisible God is made visible, hope is born anew, the Word is made flesh. And occasionally we Christians can see his glory for ourselves.

The family certainly needs to adapt, to change, to renew and perfect itself, to show God's glory more clearly. Yet even when, as now, the family seems in a mess we believe that God is in the mess. God came to live among us, God is incarnate in the family, in all families, and families appear to be an obvious channel of God's providence. God's good purposes will not be thwarted. God's Kingdom will come. This is the ground of our Christian hope that the family will survive, and it is the reason for naming *hope* as a key family value for Christians.

Taking stock

The marriage at Cana has provided a theme which runs throughout this book. It is a good story to think of as we begin to pray for the Christian family value of *hope*.

Becoming quiet

Allow your thoughts to become quiet and your body to relax.

The grace

Father, let us realize the many blessings you pour out daily through families. As we face the future, increase our hope in the power of families to express your love for us all.

The story

You will find the story of the marriage at Cana at the beginning of this book (p. vi).

Bringing it home

Where is the wedding taking place? In a fairly large room? Perhaps out of doors? Who is there—bride and groom, steward, servants, Mary the mother of Jesus, who else? Can you see Jesus and his friends, perhaps gatecrashing at the last moment? Hear the festivities. Smell the food. Taste the wine.

Now put yourself in the picture—you have plenty of characters to choose from. Who will you be? Watch Jesus as he enjoys the food and drink, toasts the bride and groom. Hear his mother whisper to him, and see her go over to the servants. Hear Jesus ask for the pots to be filled—do you feel curious? scornful, or what? See the pot water taken to the steward, and hear him praise it as fine wine—do you feel sceptical, or how do you feel? Taste some wine yourself. How does it taste? Feel the atmosphere of the party lift, and throw yourself wholeheartedly into the festivities.

Let the story unfold in your mind. Notice how you feel. Watch Jesus. When the action is over, talk to Jesus about it.

Some thoughts for today's families

Think of some of your fears about the family today. Perhaps you think of rifts or failures of responsibility in your own family. Or perhaps you worry about the future of families in general. Focus on one particular instance, and bring this one problem to Jesus. Remember what he did at Cana. Tell Jesus you trust in his power to transform the situation. Tell him you're ready to do something simple and practical to help, and ask him to show you what that is.

Think of some ways your own family loves, cares and provides for you. Thank God for his bountiful providence poured out through families all over the world.

Chapter 10

DRAW SOME OUT NOW

This book presents a vision of the Christian churches in this country exerting their power to transform family life. It is a vision of churches where people feel comfortable to admit that their family is not perfect, and where the great variety among our families is understood and valued. A vision of churches that face up to the cost of broken marriages both to individuals and to our whole society, and that decide to do something about it.

This vision sees churches which know the importance of courage in confronting pinches before they become crunches, and of perseverance in doing this again and again. Churches willing to serve families in whatever way seems most appropriate locally, but especially by helping young people to relate, by helping those marrying to clarify their values and goals and to resolve conflict, and by helping married people to cope with change.

It sees churches made glad by their ideal for marriage as a community of life and love, and sharing this ideal with joy. Churches full of hope in the family's future as a channel of God's providence, a means by which God chooses to pour abundant blessings upon humankind. And churches glimpsing in the love to be found in families of all sorts a reflection of the very life and love of God.

Once the churches have rediscovered these Christian family values, how are they to get moving and put them into practice? How can they draw from this Christian store something to transform families now?

From time to time in my parish church the Sunday homily is dropped and a letter from the bishops is read instead. These pastoral letters are meant to show the concern of the hierarchy for their flock and to address matters of current importance in the light of church tradition and teaching. Composing such letters must be a difficult art: they address people of all ages who are unknown to the bishops, and listeners of every faction and fixation in church politics can dissect every word for signs of heresy or political incorrectness and can complain to Rome or to the *News of the World* as the fancy takes them. Small wonder that pastoral letters tend to be somewhat bland and anodyne.

My rather hardworking and dedicated bishops probably have a thousand good reasons for writing as they do and not otherwise, but it was just such a letter on the pastoral care of marriage and family that caused me to daydream. What, in an ideal world, would I like to hear? How would I like them to address the church on this topic? What would scratch where I itch?

Writing your own 'pastoral letter', however short, can be a good way to clarify what you think about families. If you come from a Christian tradition that does not have a hierarchical system it may still be useful to make your own substitutions and address yourself to your own Christian church as you know it. This is the sort of letter I should like to hear read in my parish church.

It is well known that Catholics in this country think highly of marriage. Couples marrying in our churches take each other

for better, for worse
for richer, for poorer
in sickness and in health
to love and to cherish
till death ...

This is a high ideal.

Pope John Paul II has called marriage a 'community of life and love' and the family 'the domestic church'. We all recognize that it is principally through living out their calling to married love that most people find their salvation. So we value marriage highly.

In spite of struggle and difficulty many couples find great fulfilment in their marriage, and for this we thank God.
Yet in our country today marriage has become very fragile. Each year the number of divorces is a third of the number of marriages. For the young it is half.

Catholic couples are not immune from this: our marriages break as often as our neighbours'. The breakdown of a marriage brings pain and heartache to the wife and husband

going through it, to their children and to their relatives. It
harms society generally.

To us Catholics it is a challenge calling for a response. If
we set a high value upon marriage, what can we do in our
parish communities to help married people? Can a husband
and wife find among us the help that they need: help to
begin their marriage well, help to understand and adapt
to each change as their life together unfolds, help to bring
up children with wisdom and love, help to cope with trials
and difficulties expected and unexpected? Can a wife and
husband find among us realistic delight in the God-given
gifts of their marriage: delight in their sexuality, delight in
their children, delight in their anniversaries and in the
milestones of their life together? Do we recognize the joys
and pains of married people and celebrate them well in our
liturgies?

In some of our parishes awareness of the different stages
in married couples' lives is already evident. There are
marriage preparation teams, composed of young married
people who welcome every couple asking to marry in the
parish church and who show an interest in them, giving
them time to think quietly about the sort of married life
they want together and their reasons for choosing to
celebrate its start among us. There are people whose
ministry it is to *welcome young married couples* coming to live
in an area, who make a point of meeting them and inviting
them to share in appropriate parish facilities and activities.

Some parishes have *baptism groups* which help prepare
parents who bring a child to be baptized, where they look
at the impact of a new baby upon their life together as well
as at the Christian initiation they are seeking on that baby's
behalf. There are *mother and toddler groups* which offer
friendship, play space, a chance for a chat, and mutual help
and support. In many places there are *Eucharist preparation
meetings* which closely involve the parents, and which
widen their programmes so that parents can discuss the
opportunities and trials in bringing up lively boys and
girls, and can consider how to keep the married relationships
on which their children depend fresh, alive and cared for.

Parish *family groups* provide regular opportunities for
parents to discuss, to understand and to support each other.
Baby-sitting circles give parents of small children a welcome

evening out together. In some places specially trained *parish representatives* visit families with mentally disabled members to offer friendship and help. Often *Confirmation programmes* bring parents together and help them to face the challenge of their children's growing independence, as well as creating an opportunity for mutual help with what is a complex stage in many marriages.

Parish renewal is bringing many fruits, not the least of which is that in many parishes people take time to *greet each other* warmly as they assemble for the Sunday Eucharist. This can bring a sense of acceptance for wives and husbands who often do not feel at all like an ideal Christian couple: who are perhaps experiencing quarrels or disappointment or moral problems of one sort or another; whose children are perhaps unruly or disabled or socially unacceptable; whose life may seem in a mess. Throughout failure, trouble and pain married couples need to feel themselves accepted by God's people, the church, who do not simply consist of the successful and who know what it is to need forgiveness and reconciliation.

In some parishes there is a person responsible for finding *wider help for married couples*, or who can bring in experts to talk with various parish groups. There are *Engaged and Marriage Encounter* weekends which couples may attend. There is the *Catholic Marriage Advisory Council* which offers skilled marriage counselling in its centres throughout the country and has experience of helping people relate better at all stages of their lives, from the smallest children at home, through the school years and into marriage and beyond. There is the *Association of Separated and Divorced Catholics*, whose members share the pain of broken relationships and help each other so well with the daily family struggles of single parents.

Parishes which cater for the realities of married life are producing *lively liturgies* to celebrate it: prayer, song, story and symbol are used as married couples meet at different life-stages; occasions such as anniversaries, and especially silver or golden weddings, are used to renew marriage promises and to thank God for his goodness in married people's lives.

The Bishops of England and Wales ask clergy and laity to consider these examples carefully. Listen to your married people. Encourage them to speak of their daily lives, of their sorrows and of their joys. As they pass through the different stages of marriage, encourage them to meet together. At every stage help them to hear what God is saying to them *now* in their daily living and loving.

Be convinced that God is at work in their sexuality, in their self-giving, in their care and cherishing of one another, and help them to recognize God's presence.

Create an atmosphere of acceptance in which married people can admit to the inevitable strains in their relationship, and call them continually to true reconciliation. Whenever marriage seems to bring nothing but pain and anguish, remind each other that our God is no stranger to suffering and is certainly to be found alongside all who suffer.

Clergy and laity, ask yourselves: what is our parish doing? Do we help married people at different stages in their lives? Do we bring our married couples together for mutual support? Do we listen to them, accept them as they are, celebrate God's presence already among them? How could we do more? Can we adapt our parish programme to include some of the examples of good practice mentioned in this letter?

Husbands and wives, we thank God for your love one for another. May God bless you. And may the people of God who witnessed your promises help you actively to love and cherish each other until death.

If you try writing your own 'pastoral letter' in this fashion you may recognize some of the difficulties of addressing Christians of even one tradition in terms which all could accept. I have framed my letter in Roman Catholic terms and I would expect these to jump out for readers of other Christian traditions; this should make it easy to substitute your own good practice. If you do not yet know what good things for marriage and family are happening in your own church, the exercise of composing a 'pastoral letter' may spur you to find out.

I found myself wanting to go on to speak to different groups individually. Since this is a fantasy exercise, perhaps that would be permitted.

To the young

Tradition tells us the way God intends men and women to
live together—in a marriage that is faithful, lifelong and
open to new life. You inherit this tradition. A lifelong love
is still possible in marriage. It is still there for you, if you will
keep this ideal in your mind and heart. In your life you face
decisions about those you will choose as companions and
friends, and the way you will behave together. In your
choices, keep open for yourself the possibility of a lifelong
married love.

To unmarried people who have opted to live together

For the time being you are sharing a part of your lives. Care
for each other. Work for each other's true good. If you
decide to part, be straightforward and honest but try to
minimize the hurt and rejection that parting inevitably
brings. If your commitment grows, remember that the church
is ready to recognize that fact and to declare it publicly to
the community. Your local church is ready to celebrate your
relationship with a joyful wedding; if you ask them to do
so, be sure of a welcome.

To those preparing for marriage

We are glad that you are asking God's people to share in
the celebration of your life and love, and we shall try in our
churches to make that celebration all you would want it to
be. We understand that you are very busy with practical
arrangements, but we ask you to take some time in the
weeks before your wedding to look more deeply at the way
you relate together. Does your partner please and delight
you? Tell him, tell her all the qualities that gladden your
heart. Are there problems or difficulties between you? Do
not ignore them and hope they will go away, but have the
courage to talk about them and seek a solution together.
Marriage is a permanent commitment to a reconciling love;
start now to practise this daily reconciliation.

To those in marital difficulty

Marriage counsellors tell us that differences between
husband and wife are inevitable and happen in every
marriage. Please do not leave any difference to fester and to
turn your relationship sour. To ignore a problem between you,

to try to solve it individually, or by prayer alone, even to
put up with it bravely and 'offer it up': these are not *married*
ways of dealing with such problems. Jesus tells us to take
up our cross daily: for married people taking up your cross
means having the courage to take up the issue that is causing
pain between a wife and a husband and together looking
bravely for a solution. If you cannot do this without
destructiveness, remember that marriage counsellors are
specially trained to help you do it safely. Do not think that
the counsellors of the Catholic Marriage Advisory Council are
there to judge you: they carry out a ministry on behalf of
all God's people to show you the care, compassion and
understanding of Christ himself. When problems between
husband and wife are courageously tackled and resolved
they can become points of growth in a marriage and the
means of God's healing grace.

To those whose family seems different from their neighbours'

From today we shall strive to be more aware of the many
different kinds of family in which people in our countries
live. In and from these varied family settings you are called
to work out your salvation, learning to love and be loved, to
give and to receive, to care and to be cared for, to forgive
and be forgiven. In and from these varied settings we call
all families to the values of the gospel: whatever your
present family setting, go the second mile, turn the other
cheek, give your coat and your cloak as well. The church
exists to help you do it. Make sure your local church knows
of your needs. When other Christians assume that all proper
families consist of a father, mother and their children, remind
them that this is not the case. Tell them that we, your church
leaders and ministers, recognize and rejoice in the diversity
of God's people. We want them to understand and celebrate
it too.

To those who look to church leaders and ministers to understand their family difficulties

We have a duty to set before you the ideals which make for
good family life. Yet we know that, for many, family life is
far from ideal. We recognize that you often have hard choices
to make, how much you struggle and do your best, how
rarely life turns out as you had once planned. Be assured

that God is with you in your struggles. God accepts you as you are: 'You are bought and paid for.' Be assured that we recognize that you know your own circumstances best. God is pleased with all who do the best they can in their unique situation. Do not feel a second-class member of your parish community, or feel you must hide your circumstances from your brothers and sisters in Christ. Tell them that we, your church leaders and ministers, have said that we are all a pilgrim people. None of us has yet reached perfection. We look to other Christians to show you sympathy and understanding when you have hard choices to make. We do not seek to give you ready-made answers to family difficulties: we desire to show now that we understand some of the questions which you face.

Writing even a small part of your own 'pastoral letter' can help you to face up to some of the tensions between the Christian ideal of family, and families as you know them to be. Yet hierarchical instructions from the top down, however kindly meant, would be unlikely to transform family life, even if you were a bishop in the place of the present incumbent. The best use of your fantasy letter is as the basis of discussion with one or two other Christians who have attempted the same exercise. Perhaps you can agree together on just a few points, and from those can make some plans for putting Christian family values into action.

Christianity is not a solitary faith but a communal one. If you have brought your own experience to the ten gospel stories given in this book, and if you have used these gospel stories as the basis of your own prayer for today's families, you are entitled to offer your conclusions about the family to your fellow Christians and expect a sympathetic hearing. Ours is not a dead faith but a living one. Small groups of Christians sharing their convictions in this way are likely to decide to change something, however small, in their behaviour towards their own family or families in general.

Real transformation comes from the heart. I do not think we have to do much more, but we have to do some things differently. The ten Christian family values identified in this book have their source in the values of the gospel. The Year of the Family will not have been in vain if by its end little groups of Christians throughout the country can identify any of the ten values that speak to their experience, and can agree on some action which will foster that value for their own family or for families locally.

Grassroots change of this sort is irresistible. It can transform your family and the families around you. Where political and social change is needed nationally it can convince even cautious church leaders to act decisively for true Christian family values. The gospel still has power to renew the face of the earth.

This book has been about the fundamental Christian family value of *love*. Such love is quite demanding. It demands that we admit failings in our own family, recognize other families that are different from ours, and cope constructively with change. It is the kind of love which faces up to the cost of broken marriages, which says boldly that enough is enough. It is a love willing to confront pinches, resolve conflict and persevere in the desire to be reconciled. A love generous in offering service, ready to help others initiate, sustain and enrich married relationships that will last. Sometimes families can give us a glimpse of the very love of God, faithful and dependable, permanent, bountiful and creative, full of joy and hope.

Taking stock

It is fitting to end this book with a story about *love*. This story of the risen Jesus by the lake of Tiberias is told as an appendix to John's gospel. It was probably written after John's death by a disciple of the next generation—perhaps he used it to show that Jesus had risen for him, too.

Becoming quiet

Quieten your mind and relax your body.

The grace

Father, warm us by your love within our families. Help us to show love to the family you have given us.

The story

(Peter is out fishing with several disciples. They catch nothing. Jesus appears on the shore, and at his command they catch a huge netful.)

As soon as they came ashore they saw that there was some bread there, and a charcoal fire with fish cooking on it. Jesus said, 'Bring some of the fish you have just caught'. Simon Peter went aboard and dragged the net to the shore, full of big fish, one hundred and fifty-three of them; and in spite of there being so many the net was not broken. Jesus said to them, 'Come and have breakfast'. None of the disciples was bold enough to ask, 'Who are you?'; they knew quite well it was the Lord. Jesus then stepped forward, took the bread and gave it to them, and the same with the fish. This was the third time that Jesus showed himself to the disciples after rising from the dead.

After the meal Jesus said to Simon Peter, 'Simon son of John, do you love me more than these others do?' He answered, 'Yes Lord, you know I love you'. Jesus said to him, 'Feed my lambs'. A second time he said to him, 'Simon son of John, do you love me?' He replied, 'Yes, Lord, you know I love you'. Jesus said to him, 'Look after my sheep'. Then he said to him a third time, 'Simon son of John, do you love me?' Peter was upset that he asked him the third time, 'Do you love me?' and said, 'Lord, you know everything; you know I love you'.

Jesus said to him, 'Feed my sheep'.

John 21

Bringing it home

See the lake—perhaps it is a lake that you know. What is the weather? Is it grey and leaden, or is the sun sparkling on the water? See the fire on the shore, hear it crackle, feel its warmth, watch the flames flicker. Smell the fish cooking. Jesus is there preparing breakfast—what is he doing?

Then put yourself in the picture. Are you Peter, or one of the other disciples? Look at Jesus as he invites you to breakfast. How can you be so certain that he is really there? Are you hungry after your fishing trip? Enjoy the taste of the bread and the fish. As Jesus talks to Peter, remember the last time they met, when Peter denied Jesus three times. How does Peter feel? Remorseful? Ashamed? Or what? How do the others feel? Confused, perhaps or disillusioned? Hear Peter's threefold declaration of love, and Jesus' threefold commission. Tell Jesus whatever you can of your feelings.

Let the story unfold in your mind. Notice how you are feeling. Watch Jesus. When the action is over, talk to Jesus about your experience.

Some thoughts for today's families

We live in a world where people marry 'for love' and love seems to fail. Perhaps it is hard to recognize that Jesus is risen for us, too. Substitute your own name for Simon's, and hear Jesus asking you by name 'Do you love me?' Try to answer Jesus honestly and simply. Then listen to Jesus: perhaps he has a commission for you too.

What do you think Christians should be saying about family life and love? Think of a few statements that are true to your experience of families, but which reflect what you know of the bountiful love of God.

CHRISTIAN FAMILY VALUES
FOR TODAY

1. *Admitting* family failings.

2. *Recognizing* the many different types of family.

3. *Trust* during times of family change.

4. *Realism* in facing the cost of broken marriages.

5. *Courage* to confront pinches.

6. *Perseverance* in tackling pinches as they arise.

7. *Service* in helping:

   young people to relate;

   those marrying to clarify their values and goals and to manage conflict;

   married couples to cope with change.

8. *Joy* in the ideal of marriage as a community of life and love.

9. *Hope* in the future of the family as a channel of God's providence.

10. *Love* learnt and shown in families and reflecting the bountiful love of God.

FOR GROUP LEADERS

Many Christian churches are now inviting ordinary people to gather regularly to think and pray about the family. Programmes for such groups are always in demand, and this is particularly likely in a Year of the Family.

Each chapter of this book has something fresh to say about the family. Each has a theme important for families. Each identifies a value by which Christians may understand and lead family life today. Each of the ten chapters ends with a familiar gospel story which can form the basis of meditation and prayer, and which sheds light on some aspect of family life. Relevant questions can readily be added to draw out the experience of Christian groups who meet because they are concerned for the family. They will find this a user-friendly book.

The ten chapters offer ample material for one-off meetings or for short courses such as those often held during Lent. The family is an excellent subject for ecumenical meetings. Those attending are usually well in touch with their own experience of families and enjoy looking together for what Christ may be saying to them through family life.

Preparing to lead a Making Families Work course

Planning

The priest or minister is usually a key person at the planning stage. He will need a small working party to read the book and to decide how many meetings to hold and which chapters are most relevant to local people. The working party can settle the place, time and dates of the meetings.

Publicity

Meetings can be advertised with handbills and in parish newsletters in this way:

MAKING FAMILIES WORK
Six Lenten meetings

Are you happy with your family? . . . What is happening to the family today? . . . How many different sorts of family live around us? . . . How could families work better for individuals? . . . Has the family failed society or has society failed families? . . . Whatever happened to Christian family values? . . . What are the Churches doing?

Come and share your experience

Time _____   Dates _____
Place _____

The organizers could personally ask a few likely people to promise to attend. Don't forget to ask some young people, and some men. These people could then be asked to distribute handbills to friends, offering to attend with them or to give them a lift.

Preparing

Try to have the meetings in a place where people feel at home. It helps if the room is warm enough for people to take off their coats and sit comfortably. A circle of chairs is better than straight rows. Perhaps there could be a low table in the centre, with flowers and candles. Arrange for refreshments if needed.

An outline meeting

It helps if the format of each meeting is roughly similar, so that the participants get to know what to expect. To avoid repetition within the text, the parts that are the same for every meeting are given below.

Welcome

The group leader greets people as they arrive. Each person gets an *Agenda* for the meeting, with an *Ideas section* which summarizes relevant points from the chapter. Suitable Agendas and Ideas sections are reproduced after these group leaders' notes. Really organized group leaders can send these out a week before the meeting or give them out at the end of one meeting ready for the next, but then they must be prepared for people to lose or forget them.

Getting started (no more than 15 minutes)

The leader announces the *theme*, which varies with each chapter: e.g. 'Today we're going to look at the way families cope with change'. Each theme is tied to a particular *Christian family value*. The leader states this and maybe writes it up on a flipchart: e.g. 'The Christian family value we shall call on today is the value of *trust* in times of family change'.

The leader wants everyone's family experience to be valued and shared, so straightaway directs attention to the *starter question*: e.g. 'Focus on a recent loss you have undergone in your family life. What made it so hard? What, if anything, helped?' The leader invites people to think of this quietly by themselves, and then to share something of their experience with their neighbour.

Some ideas (no more than 15 minutes)

The starter question will have grounded the theme in reality. The leader then goes over the *Ideas section*, which summarizes important points from the relevant chapter of this book. If several people have read the chapter the leader can encourage a pooling of information. Those who have not read the chapter are in no way to be made to feel at a disadvantage—they are valued for their experience in families and their willingness to share it. However, if somebody is responsible for having read the chapter and goes over the salient points, everybody can then participate fully in the rest of the meeting.

Guided gospel (no more than 15 minutes)

Introduction

'Now we're going to listen to a story from the gospel to see if it sheds any light for us on these experiences of families.'

Becoming quiet

Say something like this. 'First, can I invite you to quieten your thoughts. Let your mind become still. Breathe slowly and easily. If you like, close your eyes. Let the worries and cares of the day drop away with each breath out. God is all around you. Breathe in God ...'

The grace

This varies with each meeting. Read out the grace suggested. Then say 'Perhaps you would each like to ask for this grace in your own way . . .'

The story

Introduce the story in these or similar words. 'This is a story which you probably know very well. Try hearing it today as if for the first time. Perhaps you could listen as you listen to the news, or hear it as a little child does when a story is read out loud.' For the first few meetings it helps if the leader asks someone who they know reads easily to read the story aloud to the group.

Bringing it home

Say something like 'You are going to visualize the scene in which that story is set. It doesn't have to be in biblical times or biblical clothes, so don't worry if an everyday scene comes into your mind.' The leader continues with the particular scene-setting for each meeting, which can be found, entitled 'Bringing it home', at the end of each chapter. These sections aim to leave the group members as free as possible to compose the scene for themselves, then to put themselves into the scene, choosing from a range of roles. People are reminded to notice their feelings at different points in the story, to watch Jesus and to talk to him.

Either let the story unfold. Say 'You now have five minutes of quietness. Let the story run in your mind like a film. See what happens. Keep your eye on Jesus (omit this for parables). Notice how you feel. Talk to Jesus about it.'

Or hear the story read again. Then say 'Take a few moments now to talk to Jesus about what you felt as the story was being read'.

Ending the gospel section

Say something like 'During the next week you may like to return to that story in your mind. Each time you return it may have something more to say to you.'

Group leaders should ignore the section at the end of each chapter entitled Some thoughts for today's families: these are meant for individual readers. Return to the Agenda sheets and find the *Questions* section.

Questions (no more than 15 minutes)

The questions on the Agenda sheets are triggers to draw out people's own experiences. Often it helps for people to consider a question individually, then to share what they wish with a partner, and only then to speak to the full meeting.

To do (no more than 15 minutes)

The meeting ends with suggestions for action for individuals and for groups. Encourage people to make their resolutions as specific as possible, to say exactly what they are aiming to do, who is involved, and when it will be accomplished. You may not want people to rush into ill-considered group action, but to wait until they have collected several suggestions over a period of weeks from which to choose the action which is most relevant and practical for that group. In this case it is important to note down their suggestions publicly, and to ensure that all are considered at a later date, perhaps at the final meeting.

Closing prayer

A short prayer is a good way to round off the meeting.

Agendas and Ideas sheets for individual meetings follow. These may be photocopied for group use.

Agenda 1

Getting started

Theme Searching for Christian family values.

Christian family value **Admitting** family failings.

Starter question Is there anyone you feel happy to tell exactly what your family is like, the good and the bad? If so, what makes that person easy to confide in? What makes it hard to confide in others?

Some ideas

See the Ideas section.

Guided gospel

The Pharisee and the Tax Collector—Luke 18.

Questions

Do you find other Christians understand your family difficulties? How would your local church have to change to make it easy for people to talk honestly about their family life?

Think of a category of people who you feel threaten family values—perhaps the young or the divorce-happy or unmarried mothers and fathers or homosexual people or feckless parents. Or your thoughts may run to big business or the banks or the DSS or the government. Which category of people do you consider the greatest threat to family values? How would your views have to change to become 'right with God'?

To do

For yourself During the next week try to take some small risk to be more open with others about your family circumstances. Notice whether that makes them more able to be open with you.

As a group Which single change in your church would best help people to talk more honestly about their family? Ask your group leader to note this for later action.

Closing prayer

Ideas on the search for Christian family values

It is easy to despair of the family today, yet we know we cannot go back to earlier times.

These meetings will help us to search for Christian family values for today.

We shall share our own experience of family. We accept that others may have a different experience, which we respect and value.

We shall consider stories from the gospels to see what light they can shed on family life today.

We shall look for practical ways to improve family life for ourselves and for others. We shall undertake only those actions which respect the way we experience families working.

We shall finish the course with several considered proposals from which our local church may choose the action which best serves families in our area.

Agenda 2

Getting started

Theme Defining the family.

Christian family value **Recognizing** the many different types of family.

Starter question If somebody asks you 'How's the family?' name the people you think of immediately. How are they related to you? Do they form part of your present household?

Some ideas

See Ideas section.

Guided gospel

The family of Jesus—Mark 3.

Questions

Is yours a typical family? Do you think the typical family exists? What prevents us from taking more delight in the variety of families living around us?

Most Christians feel a conflict about accepting some sorts of family. Jesus seems to ask us to have acceptance and understanding for those whose family life is less than ideal. If we do this, are we downgrading family ideals which are important to us and which we want to pass on to our children?

Perhaps there is a different conflict. There are many people for whom the ideal has not proved possible. Need they be ashamed of other Christians knowing? Do they feel the ideals should be scrapped? How do they feel about those Christians who have managed to live up to the Christian ideal of marriage?

To do

For yourself Is there anyone in your family you would like to be closer to? How about a phone call or a postcard? How about arranging to spend some time together?

As a group What single change in your church would best help all families to be accepted? Ask your group leader to note this for later action.

Closing prayer

Ideas on defining the family

Nuclear   Father, mother and their children.
We are born into a *family of origin*, we move into a *family of marriage*.

Extended   Includes grandparents and grandchildren, uncles, aunts and cousins, and other more distant relatives by blood or marriage.

Step   Includes children of a husband or wife's former marriage, the new husband or wife of a mother or father, the children of a mother's or father's former marriage.

Blended   Wife and husband in a second marriage and their children, and any of his or her children from a former marriage who live with them.

Household   Those who are living at home together and who may or may not be related.

Adoptive   Any unrelated person may be adopted as a relative by law or by custom.

Analogy   We sometimes speak of 'the parish family' or 'the family of Christians'. Religious orders and other institutions can think of themselves as families.

Three ideas One person can have many family roles—the same person can be daughter, wife, mother, aunt, cousin, grandmother etc.

One person's principal role can change over time, or new roles can be added—from son to husband to father to grandfather.

Families can be separated by death, but more often through divorce or by choice. Mostly family members are still around somewhere, but can't manage to live together.

Agenda 3

Getting started

Theme Coping with change in families.

Christian family value **Trust** during times of family change.

Starter question Focus on a recent loss you have undergone in your family life. What made it so hard? What, if anything, helped?

Some ideas

See Ideas section.

Guided gospel

The boy Jesus lost and found in the Temple—Luke 2.

Questions

Focus on a member of your family who you wish would act differently. What is the best way to invite them to change? What would help you to leave them free to make their own choice? What helps you to go on loving them whatever they do?

Are there people in your area who need help in a time of transition? New parents, perhaps, or parents of adolescents? People newly divorced or bereaved? People recently redundant or unemployed? Which group has the greatest need, or which is your church best able to help?

To do

For yourself Decide on something practical you will do during the next week to help yourself or someone close to you to go forward trustingly during a time of change.

As a group Ask your group leader to record your decisions about the group your church might best help through a time of transition.

Closing prayer

Ideas on coping with change in families

Families can go through seven life-course stages:

1 Free spirits
2 Dinkies
3 New parents
4 Adolescent family
5 Empty nester
6 Active oldies
7 Last lap

The family is at its most vulnerable when changing from one stage to the next.

Other changes arise from:
accidents
free choice
just deserts
marital breakdown.

Coping with transition cannot be rushed by effort of will. The bigger the change, the longer it takes to work through the transition.

The transition curve

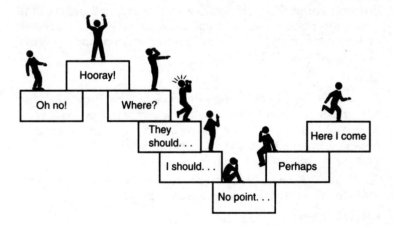

Agenda 4

Getting started

The theme The wound to the family caused by marital breakdown.

Christian family value **Realism** in facing the cost of broken marriages.

Starter question Think of a marriage that has broken down: it may be your own, it may be that of someone you love. Think of all the high hopes at the beginning of the marriage, photographs of good times, expectations of being loved and cherished, happy and successful. Is it hard to look squarely at the ruin of those hopes? What hurts or disappoints the most? What is lost and can never be recovered? What, if anything, helped you through?

Some ideas

See Ideas section.

Guided gospel

The merciful father—Luke 15.

Questions

Think of some ways mass divorce affects society: the damage to children, the effect on health and well-being, the pressure on housing and welfare and grant-giving services. What experience do you have of this? Can we as a society do anything about it?

Is your church exempt from mass divorce? How are you already supporting those going through this unhappy process? How could you do better?

To do

For yourself During the week turn to God, your Father. Tell him how much you mind about any particular marriage that has broken. Admit that as a society we are in a mess, that we are finding it impossible to live in love. Ask God to show you in time what you can do to help.

As a group Ask your group leader to note for later action your ideas for ways to help newly divorced people.

Closing prayer

Ideas on marital breakdown: the family wounded

If marriage is the cement holding families together, the breakdown of marriage wounds families and causes them to fall apart.

One marriage in three in this country currently ends in divorce, and it is estimated that 40 per cent of existing marriages will do so. Britain has the third highest rate after the USA and Russia, but all Western countries have high rates.

Committed Christians divorce rather less frequently than other people, but nominal Christians divorce as often as the rest.

Marriage used to be viewed as a *contract*, with clear roles and duties. Now it is considered a *covenant* of life and love. This is a high ideal, but can raise expectations of happiness which often are not met.

Agenda 5

Getting started

The theme Recognizing and resolving pinches.

Christian family value **Courage** to confront pinches.

Starter question What do you understand by a pinch? (Take a quick look at the top of the Ideas section.) Can you think of a pinch you feel right now? What, in your experience, makes it difficult to take up pinches with the person causing them?

Some ideas

See Ideas section.

Guided gospel

Continue the story of the merciful father—Luke 15.

Questions

If you have made marriage vows and have managed to keep them you have something in common with the elder son who never once disobeyed his father's orders. Do you share any of the older son's feelings when you think about those who don't keep their vows today? If you've not been able to keep your marriage vows, what do you feel about those who have? If you have never married, what do you feel about both groups?

Could your church help couples getting married to recognize and resolve pinches? Could they do this for married couples? Or any other groups?

To do

For yourself Can you resolve to take up some pinch with the person causing it?

As a group Ask the group leader to record the group which your church is best able to help with resolving pinches.

Closing prayer

Ideas about recognizing and resolving pinches

A pinch is a situation where one person in a relationship feels at odds with the way the other is behaving. The other person seems not to notice anything wrong.

It is not enough to forgive the person causing the pinch. Pinches do not go away by themselves.

In any close relationship the person feeling the pinch must go beyond forgiveness, take up the pinch and deal with it.

In a marriage this means telling your partner and helping them to understand the problem. It requires the partner to be ready to listen and understand. Then husband and wife must work together to find a solution.

Resolving pinches strengthens marriages. Unresolved pinches cause a build-up of unhappiness that puts a marriage at risk.

Agenda 6

Getting started

The theme How a marriage works or fails.

Christian family value **Perseverance** in confronting every pinch as it occurs.

Starter question Can you think of any instance where defending or blaming made it impossible to resolve a problem?

Some ideas

See Ideas section.

Guided gospel

Jesus cures the paralysed man—Mark 2.

Questions

Many married couples do not realize that they need not lie helplessly paralysed by their problems. It is often possible to take them up and deal with them. Can you think of a pinch you took up and resolved successfully?

Some people with troubled marriages may need to ask a counsellor they can trust to help them find healing. Who could they approach? What would be needed to get them there?

To do

For yourself During the next week, can you act when appropriate as a forgiven person, cutting out the blame and the defence? Can you go on practising taking up pinches and resolving them?

As a group How can your church group help people with troubled marriages to get professional help?

Closing prayer

Ideas about how marriages work

If one partner feels a pinch, and raises and resolves it, a marriage grows stronger.

Ignoring pinches does not make them go away.

Pinches continually ignored can lead to a crunch, a really unhappy marriage.

Crunches are felt by both partners.

Kissing and making-up does not get a couple out of a crunch. Only facing and resolving their conflicts can do that.

Marriage counsellors are trained to help couples to resolve their conflicts safely.

Unresolved crunches end either in divorce or separation, or in a marriage that falls far short of a community of life and love.

Agenda 7

Getting started

The theme What can Christian communities do to help married people live in love?

Christian family value **Service** to the married relationship.

Starter question At what stage do you think marriages are the most vulnerable: Preparing for marriage? When the first baby arrives? With young children? With adolescents? After the children leave? Any other time?

Some ideas

See Ideas section.

Guided gospel

Jesus washes his disciples' feet—John 13.

Questions

Think of the people in a family that you know. What corns, blisters and sores have they collected on their journey? How might you help them feel understood and restored?

How could your parish hall or facilities be better used to help families?

What marriage preparation is on offer for couples marrying in your local church? Is it what couples like and need?

What has your parish got by way of baptism and confirmation programmes? Do people enjoy these? Do they find them helpful? Do the organizers need any extra help?

What are the needs of young parents near you? Can you do anything to meet these needs?

What can you find out about parenting programmes?

To do

For yourself Pick something from the Ideas sheet to work on during the week.

As a group Where best can your church group put its efforts for families?

Closing prayer

Ideas for helping married people to live in love

Bear in mind ...

Political action What are we doing as voters, council tax payers, members of political parties?

Social action What are we doing as members of charitable and self-help organizations, as fundraisers for good causes and as good neighbours?

Liturgical action What are we doing in our liturgies to celebrate married love?

But be sure to add ...

Helping people to relate well

—as young people
How do we help them at home to have self-esteem? To show affection? To sort out quarrels? To learn about sex? To treat others fairly? Is there an adequate programme at school for social and personal education?

—as young people about to marry
How do we help them: clarify their values; share out their roles; manage conflict?

—as married people
How do we help them: cope with change; persevere in sorting out pinches; keep love alive?

Agenda 8

Getting started

The theme Where is God in married life?

Christian family value Joy in the ideal of Christian marriage as a community of life and love.

Starter question Do married people on the whole look very joyful? Can you recall seeing true joy shining out of a married couple?

Some ideas

See Ideas section.

Guided gospel

Jesus is transfigured—Matthew 17.

Questions

Did you remember seeing true joy shine out of a married couple?

If you are married, can you think of an instance of real joy that you shared with your partner? Do you agree that such experiences can give us a glimpse of God's love?

In the hard, everyday world of married life, can you think of instances of sustaining, healing, and helping each other grow? How could these reveal the Trinity at work?

How can we keep hold of the vision of the joy and love of marriage? How can we show this vision to those around us? Can we pass this vision on to the young?

To do

For yourself What single change in your life, however small, would help you or those around you to rejoice in the ideal of Christian marriage as a community of life and love? A show of affection? A special meal or a party? A special liturgy? More time spent at home? Getting rid of time-wasting engagements? Quality time with your partner? What change would be best in your circumstances? What would help you to make that change?

As a group How would you like your church group to celebrate the joy and love of marriage?

Closing prayer

Ideas for finding God in married life

All married couples can think of some special moments in their life together. Significant. Outside time. These can give us a glimpse of what is ultimately special, significant, outside time. They are glimpses of God.

Marriages last where couples sustain each other, heal each other and help each other grow. In such marriages we catch sight of the Father and Sustainer of all, of the Son and Healer, and of the Spirit and Growth-giver.

Married couples are called daily to reconciliation. They are called to forgive each other, and then to go beyond forgiveness to repentance, change and renewal. This is God's work: 'Now I am making the whole of creation new' (Revelation 21).

Lifelong love in marriage is still possible. It is God's desire for us, and it reflects God's great love which has no end. We need to believe in this ideal with all our heart.

Agenda 9

Getting started

The theme The family as domestic church.

Christian family value **Hope** in the future of the family as a channel of God's providence.

Starter question What is your first reaction to hearing the family described as 'the domestic church'. Could the words 'domestic church' possibly fit your own family?

Some ideas

See Ideas section.

Guided gospel

The marriage at Cana—John 2.

Questions

Do you think any particular model of the family fits the way your own works? Could some of the conflicts in your family arise because different members have different models of what the family should be?

The Christian church strives to be catholic or universal, to cater for all its members. So does the family. Does your experience of church tell you anything about how families can live together?

To do

For yourself Think of some of your fears about the family today. Perhaps you think of rifts or failures of responsibility in your own family. Or perhaps you worry about the future of families in general. Focus on one particular instance. During the week bring this one problem to Jesus. Remind yourself of what he did at Cana. Tell Jesus you trust in his power to transform the situation. Tell him you're ready to do something simple and practical to help, and ask him to show you what that is.

As a group What single change for your church group would best help families? Ask your group leader to record your ideas.

Closing prayer

Ideas about the family as domestic church

The church can be seen as ...

An institution —established by Christ, with clear rules and roles

A community —the people of God, or the body of Christ with its different parts working together

A sacrament —a sign of God's activity

A herald —proclaiming God's word

A servant —spreading justice, love and peace.

Families can be ...

Institutions —legally recognized, with clear rules and roles

Communities —living together with a sense of belonging

Sacraments —showing and celebrating (God's) love and providence

Heralds —teaching, communicating and prophesying (telling it like it is)

Servants —interested in the wider world, generous and charitable to all.

Christians can sometimes see that the family is already alive with God's presence. From this perspective:

Every please and thank you and sorry and wow! becomes family *prayer*.

Opening our hearts to each other becomes family *gospel*.

Work, service, hugs and kisses, and especially sexual intercourse between wife and husband, become family *Eucharist*: 'This is my body given for you.'

Agenda 10

Getting started

The theme Reconciling real and ideal families.

Christian family value **Love** learnt and shown in families and reflecting the bountiful love of God.

Starter question If the leaders of your church came to ask you what your family life is like, how would you reply?

Some ideas

See Ideas section.

Guided gospel

The risen Jesus with Peter by the lake—John 21.

Questions

What would you like your own church leaders and ministers to say about families? Agree on a few sentences that are true to what you believe and to your own experience of the way families work.

To do

For yourself We live in a world where people marry 'for love' and love seems to fail. Perhaps it is hard to recognize that Jesus is risen for us, too. During the next days and weeks try substituting your own name for Simon's, and hear Jesus asking you by name 'Do you love me?' Try to answer Jesus honestly and simply. Listen to what Jesus says next. Perhaps he has a commission for you too.

As a group Look at all the action to support families which you have identified since the first meeting. Which is the most needed and the most practical for your church group? Can you help your church to start some service to families that will endure and meet a real need?

Closing prayer

Ideas on reconciling real and ideal families

We look to our Christian leaders and ministers to put before us ideals about family life. We also expect them to be realistic, to reflect family life as we know it, and to show us where God is in our own experience of family. Are we asking too much?

Maybe after these meetings we ourselves are better able to shed false ideals, to hold on to ideals that are true, and to find God in our real family life.

REFERENCES

Chapter 1

p.5 'Those who are baptized or are nominal believers in their faith are no different in the outcome of their marriage from those who have no faith': J. Dominian, *Make or Break* (SPCK, 1984).

Chapter 2

p.11 In 1990 the proportion of households consisting of a 'traditional' family of a married or cohabiting couple with dependent children was only 25 per cent. Source: *General Household Survey* (OPCS, 1991).

Chapter 3

p.15 This classification follows that of Sue Waldrond-Skinner, *Family Matters* (SPCK, 1988), which is based on work by E. Carter and M. McGoldrick, *The Family Life Cycle* (Gardner Press, 1980). I have chosen titles for each stage which reflect the viewpoint of a key couple as they pass through the successive stages.

p.22 (also p.105) The illustration of the transition curve is redrawn from Maggie Smith, *Changing Course* (Mercury Communications, 1992). It is an adaptation of J. Adams, J. Hayes and B. Hopson's transition curve from *Transition* (Martin Robertson, 1976).

Chapter 4

p.29 P. L. Berger and H. Kellner, *Marriage and the Construction of Reality* (Diogenes, 1964).

p.29 J. Bernard, *The Future of Marriage* (Yale University Press, 1973).

pp.29 and 30 Persons divorcing in England and Wales per 1,000 married people:

1961	2.1
1971	6.0
1981	11.9
1990	12.9

Source: *Social Trends* (HMSO, 1993)

p.30 P. Mansfield and J. Collard, *The Beginning of the Rest of Your Life* (Macmillan, 1988).

p.31 'Religious affiliation in itself is no protection. . . . It is the commitment and practice of a faith that disapproves of divorce which is protective': J. Dominian, *Make or Break* (SPCK, 1984).

pp.31–2 J. Dominian, *Passionate and Compassionate Love* (Darton, Longman & Todd, 1991).

Chapter 5

p.37 G. Egan, *The Skilled Helper* (Brooks Cole, 1991).

Chapter 6

p.45 M. Grimer, *Water Made Wine* (Darton, Longman & Todd, 1986); M. Grimer, *Making Marriage Work* (Geoffrey Chapman, 1987).

p.46 A. Freud, *The Ego and the Mechanisms of Defence* (Hogarth Press, 1966).

Chapter 7

p.59 J. Dominian, *Passionate and Compassionate Love* (1991).

p.60 M. Vincent, *Love Needs Learning* (Geoffrey Chapman, 1994).

Chapter 8

pp.66–70 The scheme for training parish marriage preparation teams is elaborated in M. Grimer, *Water Made Wine* (Darton, Longman & Todd, 1986).

Chapter 9

p.74 Pope John Paul II, *Familiaris Consortio* (Catholic Truth Society, 1981).

p.76 A. Dulles, *Models of the Church* (Gill and Macmillan, 1987).

Geoffrey Chapman Pastoral Studies Series

Making RCIA work, handling the management of change and loss, parish evangelization, diocesan renewal, moral theology at the end of the twentieth century, the challenges raised by *Christifideles Laici*, reconciliation, these are all issues to be covered in the Geoffrey Chapman Pastoral Studies series.

For the clergy, pastoral workers and interested lay people, the series is based on experience, and provides a comprehensive introduction to the issues involved.

The authors are recognized authorities on their subjects and bring their considerable experience and expertise to bear on the series.

ALREADY PUBLISHED IN THE SERIES:

Grieving for Change:
A Spirituality for Refounding Gospel Communities
Gerald Arbuckle SM

Called to Mission:
A Workbook for the Decade of Evangelization
Christine Dodd

Making RCIA Work:
An Anthology of Material for Use in RCIA Groups
Christine Dodd

Making Families Work:
A New Search for Christian Family Values
Margaret Grimer

New Directions in Moral Theology:
The Challenge of Being Human
Kevin T. Kelly